Robes,
Blankets,
and Beads

THE CIVILIZATION OF THE AMERICAN INDIAN SERIES

Rifles, Blankets, and Beads

Identity, History, and the Northern Athapaskan Potlatch

By William E. Simeone

University of Oklahoma Press
Norman

Published with the assistance of the National Endowment for the Humanities, a federal agency which supports the study of such fields as history, philosophy, literature, and language.

Library of Congress Cataloging-in-Publication Data

Simeone, William E.
   Rifles, blankets, and beads : identity, history, and the northern Athapaskan potlatch / by William E. Simeone.
       p.   cm.—(The civilization of the American Indian series; v. 216)
   Includes bibliographical references and index.
   ISBN: 978-0-8061-3508-3 (paper)
   1. Athapaskan Indians—Social life and customs.   2. Potlatch. I. Title. II. Series.
   E99.A86S57   1995
   979.8'0904972—dc20   94-48470
                                                                CIP

Rifles, Blankets, and Beads: Identity, History, and the Northern Athapaskan Potlatch is Volume 216 in The Civilization of the American Indian Series.

The paper in this book meets the guidelines for permanence and durability of the Committee on Production Guidelines for Book Longevity of the Council on Library Resources, Inc. ♾

To
Bill & Jane
And
Martha & Oscar

Contents

Illustrations

PHOTOGRAPHS

TABLES

MAPS

Preface

I first went to live in the Athapaskan village of Tanacross, Alaska, in 1971. I had been sent there to perform alternative service as a lay worker for the Episcopal Church. I was twenty-two years old. For eighteen months my former wife, Carolyn, and I lived and worked in the community. During this period we developed friendships that have endured for more than twenty years. In the summer of 1976, Carolyn and I built a house in the village that we lived in for two years before moving to Anchorage. While living in Anchorage, we returned frequently to the village for visits that lasted from a few days to several months. When in 1986 I had to select a topic for my doctoral dissertation, Tanacross seemed an inevitable choice.

My announced intention to do research produced mixed reactions from people in the village. Most encouraged me and participated in the project, but others were wary. They distrusted anthropologists and expressed the view that we "make money off of Indians." Some, including my mentor and best friend, said no book would help the Alaska Natives. Aware of these views, I finished my research and in time completed the manuscript.

When I circulated the manuscript among several friends in the village, I got various reactions. Some were favorable, and some were not. One person, for example, took exception to my description of events surrounding the selection of the chief in 1912. I had based it on missionary accounts that indicated the chief was chosen through an election organized by the missionaries. The villager maintained that the chief had inherited his position from his father. A more general complaint arose from the fact that I have written about individuals who are still living and are recognizable, despite my use of pseudonyms. To talk (or by extension, write) about people is considered *injih,* or bad luck, and bad manners. Moreover, some people do not agree with my interpretation of the potlatch or the fact that I have written about the ceremony at all. For them, the potlatch is a very personal and spiritual event. As one person put it, "The potlatch is our life." The ceremony, they feel, has nothing to do with politics or with non-Native people. As one might imagine, I was gratified by the encouraging responses to my manuscript and sensitive to the strictures of critics.

The issues I endeavor to address in this book are, I believe, important to everyone concerned with American Indian people. There is a prevalent view that contemporary American Indian people have no culture and that they exist in limbo, suspended between their past and the modern world. No longer able or wanting to live in the past and cut off from the present, American Indian people have been relegated to the margins of American history and American society. In attempting to rectify this situation, non-Natives have consistently illuminated the enormous problems that beset American Indians: high rates of suicide, alcoholism, child and spouse abuse, and chronic unemployment. While these problems cannot be ignored, to focus only on them misses the dynamic integrity of contemporary American Indian cultures. We need, as Ann Fienup-Riordan (1992: 20) points out, to identify not only the problems but also the solutions that have enabled many American Indian individuals and communities to preserve a positive sense of community identity in spite of overwhelming odds.

Community rituals such as the potlatch and the "tradition bearers" are affirmative aspects of modern Athapaskan life. Both provide a positive sense of identity through a synthesis of the past with the present. The potlatch, in spite of efforts by misguided but well-intentioned critics to destroy it, survives as an expression of community vitality and traditional values. Tradition bearers chart the future for their people. In doing so, they try to maintain a symmetry between the old and the new, a melding of the past with the present and a path that leads away from destruction to harmony. On the village level this is a matter not simply of fulfilling institutional roles but of creating leadership out of personal experience and an understanding of their culture. Because of the tradition bearers, Athapaskan culture has not disappeared: it exists today and will continue into the future.

This book is an ethnographic description, analysis, and interpretation of the culture and history of the Tanacross people. The contents are based on my observations and research that began in 1971, but most of the data were collected between December 1986 and November 1987. I lived in my own house in the village but visited people on a regular basis. During my visits I collected information through conversations and "active" participant observation (Nelson 1969). Data collected from conversations were recorded either during the conversation or immediately afterward. Formal interviews, some of which were tape-recorded, were conducted with all village elders. Besides talking to people, I went on winter and fall trips to hunt moose, joined a village fire crew, cut and hauled cordwood, and attended potlatches. Before conducting fieldwork in 1987, I had attended approximately twenty-five potlatches. During the course of my most recent research, I attended another six ceremonies, three in Tanacross and three in other villages. At potlatches I participated in a number of activities including the preparation and serving of food and helping to build grave fences.

WILLIAM E. SIMEONE

Anchorage, Alaska

Acknowledgments

Numerous people contributed to this book. First and fore-
most, I am grateful to the people of Tanacross. I am especially
indebted to my "second parents," Martha and Oscar Isaac,
who saw me through a very difficult time, and to my brothers
and sisters, Rose, Edward, Jerry, Marion, Cora, Lee, and
Sharon. Thanks also go to my good friends Julius and Rica
Paul, Brittan and Dolly Jonathan, Gaither and Bee Paul, Bob
Jonathan, Emma Jonathan, Kenneth and Ellen Thomas, Al-
fred and Mildred Jonathan, Alice Brean, and Titus David of
Tetlin.

I want to remember Grandma Jenny, Annie Denny, Steven
Northway, Charlie James, Andrew and Maggie Isaac, and
Silas Solomen.

Paul Milanowski, James Kari, and Michael Krauss provided
information on the spelling of words in the Tanacross language. A special acknowledgment goes to Matt O'Leary, who
provided the maps. Others who have provided support and
encouragement are David Damas, Richard Preston, Richard
Slobodin, and especially Harvey Feit. Without Professor Feit's
persistence and support this book may never have come to
pass. Catherine McClellan provided many useful and insight-
ful comments on the manuscript. I hope I have been able to
come close to her standard of excellence. As external readers,
Charles Bishop, John Cook, and Jim VanStone provided

useful criticisms and encouragement. Special thanks go to Jim for his encouragement and friendship over these many years. I owe an intellectual debt to Sergie Kan. Of course, any mistakes are mine alone.

I am also indebted to Tom Dunk, Eudene Luther, Taylor Brelsford, and Kerry Feldman for long talks that helped me to disentangle my thoughts, I also want to thank Walter and Connie VanHorn for their support.

A large debt of gratitude goes to my wonderful parents, Jane and Bill, for their editorial comments and unwavering support and to my daughters, Delia and Jessica. I also want to thank Rose for being there.

Research would have been impossible without financial help from the School of Graduate Studies, McMaster University. Research at the Episcopal Church Archives was supported by a grant from the Alaska Historical Commission. The Anchorage Museum of History and Art provided office space during early phases of the research. My friend and employer Steve Braund generously provided computer facilities and time to complete the manuscript.

During the course of the project I was fortunate to be able to hire Larry Jonathan as a research assistant. In his early thirties, Larry is fluent in the Tanacross language and is considered by almost everyone in the village to be very knowledgeable about Tanacross culture. He provided considerable insight into the meaning of the potlatch, and he is one of the few young men who has hosted his own potlatch. Larry not only helped me to understand something about Tanacross culture and the potlatch but was also of considerable help in keeping my spirits up during some difficult times. I thank him here.

W.E.S.

Introduction

Anthropologists and laypeople alike have been consistently fascinated by the splendid ceremonial distribution of gifts known as the potlatch. For the most part, the public is aware of potlatches held by the Tlingit, Haida, Tsimshian, and Kwakiutl people living along the Northwest Coast of North America. Relatively less is known about similar ceremonies practiced by Northern Athapaskan people living in the interior of Alaska and the eastern Yukon Territory. This book is about the potlatch as practiced by the Tanacross people, a group of Athapaskan-speaking people living in the Upper Tanana Region of east-central Alaska.

The potlatch is a public distribution of gifts that commemorates a particular event in a person's life or heals a tear in the social fabric (Guedon 1974, 1981; McClellan 1975; McKennan 1959). Gifts are distributed, for example, on the occasion of a young person's first successful hunt, to celebrate the return of a person after a long absence or recovery from an acute illness, or to honor someone, such as a spouse. People also distribute gifts as restitution for an injury or insult and even for an offense as grievous as murder. Usually the most compelling reason for holding a potlatch is the death of an individual.

The purpose of this book is to describe and interpret the meaning of the contemporary Athapaskan potlatch within a historical context. To do this I examine four interrelated

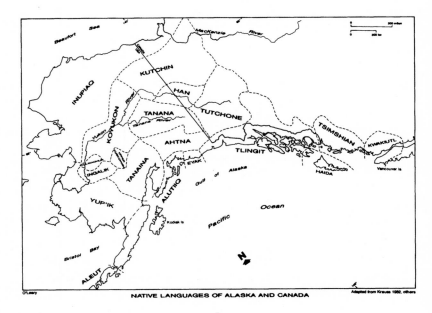

NATIVE LANGUAGES OF ALASKA AND CANADA

topics under the overarching theme of the dynamic between competition and cooperation. These topics are the introduction of trade goods into Athapaskan culture, leadership, the problem of cultural identity, and the potlatch.

In Athapaskan culture, competition and cooperation exist in a dialectical relationship. Individuals compete for power and prestige in the face of a cultural ideal that stresses cooperation or solidarity.[1] In the context of political and economic domination, however, competition is reshaped into a symbol for the white man and cooperation becomes a symbol for unity and Indianness. The resulting ideology, the "Indian way," becomes a critique of things the way they are and a vision of the way things should be.[2]

Some scholars have argued that American Indian involvement in the fur trade collapsed the dialectical relationship
between cooperation and competition as individual trappers
began to work for their own self-interest. Indicative of this
change was the use of trade goods in the potlatch. Irving
Goldman (1975), for example, argued that the distribution of
trade goods in the Kwakiutl potlatch wholly subverted the
meaning of the ceremony so that it became "Christianized
and commercialized" (Goldman 1975: 12–13). As a result, the
modern Kwakiutl potlatch is a "survival," undermined by the
concept of "alienated wealth" that altered the significance of
the ceremony from an expression of community to an arena
for individual rivalry. This was also the fate of the Athapaskan potlatch, according to Robert A. McKennan (1959)
and Stephen Strong (1972). In their view, access to trade
goods created a milieu for the development of a prestige
economy based on accumulation and competitive redistribution in the potlatch. Their analysis, however, ignores the
point that trade goods are transformed into gifts by the very
act of distribution (Gregory 1982). Rather than remaining
alienated goods, or symbolic of the conceptual system of the
dominant society, trade goods were given meanings that
reflected the indigenous cultural system.

The dynamic between cooperation and competition, in
significant measure, revolves around the issue of leadership.
Because of their social position, "old-time chiefs" were effec-
tively able to exploit the developing trade to accumulate
wealth. As their wealth increased so did their ability to hold
large, ostentatious potlatches that enhanced their individual
prestige (Fall 1987; McClellan 1975; McKennan 1959, 1969;
Strong 1972; Townsend 1965, 1975). For some Athapaskan
groups, such as the Carrier (Bishop 1983, 1987) and the

Tutchone and Tagish (McClellan 1975), these transformations led to the development of a stratified society with inherited leadership and clan crests modeled after their coastal neighbors.[3]

Certainly participation in the fur trade enabled leaders to enhance their individual prestige through the distribution of trade goods. Authority, however, did not rest only on prestige garnered through the distribution of exotic or scarce goods in the potlatch. A leader's position within society also depended on his knowledge of supernatural power, his ability to organize and motivate the people in subsistence production, his sib affiliation, and his generosity (Fall 1987). In the contemporary culture, leadership is divided between young, Western-educated leaders who administer the village and tradition bearers whose primary role is to lead in the potlatch. Like leaders in the past, tradition bearers compete to enhance their individual prestige through the public demonstration of traditional knowledge and the ability to organize and motivate the people. As bearers of tradition, however, they are expected to maintain a model of Athapaskan cultural identity, which stresses cooperation. This dynamic is rooted in the historical culture, but a key to its current dimensions lies in understanding the nature of contemporary cultural identity.

In the literature on contemporary potlatches, the issue of cultural identity has been addressed by Mary Lee Stearns (1975), who argues that the Haida, as a colonized people, can only maintain their distinctiveness on the symbolic level. Through the potlatch the Haida reinforce their cultural identity by setting themselves apart from non-Natives through an assertion of "norms" that stress unity, equality, and cooperation (ibid., 163). The exchange of gifts maintains community solidarity, while reciprocity continues to define and symbolize the individual's membership in the group, thus producing a sense of unity. Despite their insistence on equality, the Haida are competitive. In public this rivalry is suppressed through the reaffirmation of mutual indebtedness and distribution of gifts to all guests, which "nourishes the current myth that 'everyone works together'" (ibid., 164). Stearns stresses the development of the Haida potlatch as an expression and maintenance of culturally meaningful action in the context of political and economic domination. Her analysis is limited, though, to the extent that she views the Haida ceremony as nurturing a sense of identity completely "insulated" from non-Natives (ibid., 166).

Like the Haida, Tanacross people compete with non-Natives on an ideological and rhetorical level (Schwimmer 1972). In the Athapaskan potlatch public competition is submerged under an assertion of cultural values that stress cooperation. Contemporary Athapaskan identity, however, is not nurtured in isolation from non-Natives. It is a product of the dynamic relationship between Natives and non-Natives. As such, it exists in a never-ending set of images Native people have of themselves and of non-Natives. These images revolve around the oppositions of competition and cooperation, as well as past and present, Indian and non-Indian. Competition, seen as self-centered behavior and jealousy, is attributed to non-Natives. Cooperation, seen as sharing, reciprocity, love, respect, kinship, and competence, is symbolic of the Indian way and the traditional hunting life. The latter are the images that Native people consider "real" and to have existed only in the traditional past. The key arena for maintaining and reproducing these images is the potlatch.

In the potlatch the people attempt to re-create a model for social behavior that reflects and restates the ideal of the

Indian way. For the elders and leadership of the community, these values constitute an alternative model of social relations in which the individual acquires meaning within the context of a web of relationships. It is therefore a statement against the individualism of non-Native society. The potlatch is also a drama in which these relationships are formalized and carried through in the rituals of feasting, dancing and singing, oratory, and the distribution of gifts.

Rifles,
Blankets,
and Beads

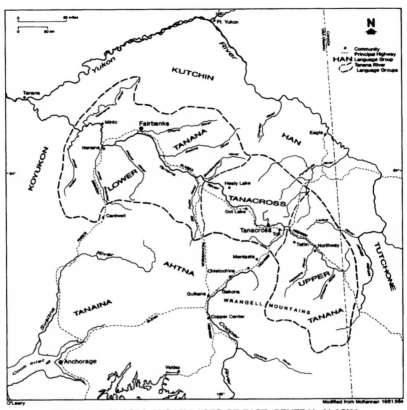

NATIVE LANGUAGES AND VILLAGES OF EAST-CENTRAL ALASKA

CHAPTER 1

The Village and Its Setting

Tanacross is located in the Upper Tanana Region of east-central Alaska between the Tanana River and the Alaska Highway, 100 miles west of the Alaska–Canada border. Tok Junction, the regional center, is 10 miles east of the village at the junction of the Alaska and Glenn highways. Fairbanks, the nearest urban center, is 200 miles to the northwest. There are four other Athapaskan villages in the region: Healy Lake, Dot Lake, Tetlin, and Northway. To the south, in the valley of the Copper River, are the villages of Mentasta, Chistochina, Gakona, Gulkana, and Copper Center. All of these villages, along with the communities of Minto and Nenana, participate in potlatches with the Tanacross people.

THE NATURAL ENVIRONMENT

From its source in the Wrangell Mountains to its confluence with the Yukon, the Tanana River is 440 miles long. The river is fed by glacial runoff discharged from the Wrangells to the south. Silt in the runoff makes the river gray and opaque. North of the river are the rolling hills of the Yukon–Tanana uplands with elevations ranging from 2,000 to 6,000 feet. Cutting through these hills are the

Table 1
1990 Census Figures for the Tanana River and Copper River Communities

Settlement	Population
Dot Lake	70
Chistochina	60
Copper Center	449
Gakona	163
Gulkana	103
Healy Lake	47
Mentasta	96
Minto	218
Nenana	393
Northway	123
Tanacross	106
Tetlin	87
Tok	935

Source: U.S. Census, Alaska Department of Labor, 1991.

clear-water tributaries of the Fortymile, Charley, Goodpaster, Salcha, and Ladue rivers. South of the Tanana lie the glaciated flanks of the Nutzotin Range and the Mentasta Mountains, with elevations ranging from 3,000 to 8,000 feet. Farther to the south are the Wrangells and the Alaska Range with peaks over 16,000 feet (Marcotte 1991: 13). The climate is continental, with warm, lush summers, extreme winters, and low precipitation.

Everywhere are miles of forest. White spruce (*Picea glauca*) and paperbirch (*Betula papyrifera*) are found in the well-drained areas, and black spruce (*Picea mariana*), balsam poplar (*Populus balsamifera*), willow (*Salix* sp.), and alder are found in the swampy regions. Above 3,500 feet are low brush and alpine tundra. Bog blueberries (*Vaccinium uliginosum*) and highbush cranberries (*V. vitis-idaea*) are plentiful in the late summer and early fall. There are also alpine berries (*Arctostaphylos alpina*), crowberries or blackberries (*Empetrum nigrum*), raspberries (*Rubus idaeus*), rosehips (*Rosa acicularris*), Labrador or Hudson's Bay tea (*Ledum groenlandicum*), and wild rhubarb (*Polyganum alaskanum*) (ibid., 14).

Big game animals found in the Upper Tanana Region include moose (*Alces alces*), Dall sheep (*Ovis dalli*), black (*Ursus americanus*) and brown bears (*U. arctos*), and caribou (*Rangifer tarandus*), which aggregate into several named herds: the Fortymile, the Mentasta, the Nabesna, and the Nelchina. Furbearers of significance include hare (*Lepus americanus*), lynx (*Felis canadenis*), marten (*Martes americanus*), wolf (*Canis lupus*), wolverine (*Gulo gulo*), red fox (*Vulpes vulpes*), beaver (*Castor canadensis*), ermine (*Mustela erminea*), and the stately muskrat (*Ondatna zibethicus*). There are also porcupines (*Erethizon dorsatum*). Large numbers of ducks, swans, and geese also appear seasonally. The varieties of fish include broad whitefish (*Coregonus nasus*), humpback whitefish (*C. pidshian*), Arctic grayling (*Thymallus arcticus*), northern pike (*Esox lucius*), longnose sucker (*Catostomus catostomus*), and burbot (*Lota lota*). Few salmon ascend the Tanana past the mouth of the Goodpaster, so these fish are unavailable to residents of the Upper Tanana Region. Salmon are plentiful in the Copper River, and residents of the region travel south to get chinook or king salmon (*Oncorhynchus tshawytscha*), coho or silver salmon (*O. kisutch*), and sockeye or red salmon (*O. nerka*)(Marcotte 1991).

TANACROSS

Tanacross draws its name from a ford in the river called Tanana Crossing. The crossing was used by travelers on the Eagle trail, which connected Valdez with Eagle on the Yukon River. Originally, the village was called Tanana Crossing or simply the "crossing," but in the 1930s the name was changed to Tanacross because people confused it with Tanana, a village located at the mouth of the Tanana River. The Tanacross people speak the Tanacross language, which belongs to the Athapaskan family of languages spoken by American Indian people scattered throughout northwestern North America and as far south as California, New Mexico, and Arizona (Krauss and Golla 1981). Northern Athapaskan is spoken by a number of groups living in Alaska and western Canada. Neighboring groups of the Tanacross are the Han, the Ahtna, the Tanana, and the Upper Tanana.

Native inhabitants of the Tanana River drainage are collectively known as Tanana Athapaskans (McKennan 1981). Historically, they were organized into a number of bands that, according to McKennan (ibid., 562), had no self-defined tribal identity but thought of themselves as localized groups that constituted both social and geographic units. Often contiguous bands were sufficiently connected through marriage, geography, and common interest that they considered themselves a larger group or regional band. The Tanacross people are descendants of the Mansfield-Ketchumstuk band, which resided principally in the villages of Mansfield, Dih thaad or Dixthada, and Ketchumstuk. Their nearest neighbors, the Upper Tanana-speaking people of Tetlin and Northway, were organized into three bands: the Tetlin–Last Tetlin band, the Lower Nabesna–Scottie Creek band, and the Upper

Nabesna–Upper Chisana band. To the west was the Healy River–Joseph band, some of whose descendants now live in Healy Lake. The people of these bands were similar in custom and connected through intermarriage (McKennan 1969, 1981; Guedon 1974).

Hoping to attract Native people from all of these groups, the Episcopal Church began a mission at Tanana Crossing in 1912. The location was selected because it was thought to be centrally located, and the Church was able to purchase the abandoned Signal Corps buildings already on the site. Initially, the mission was only moderately successful as the Native people found it difficult to live a sedentary existence, since their life was centered on seasonal movements to hunt, fish, and trap. As a result, Mansfield and Ketchumstuk people visited the mission irregularly and the other bands in the region hardly did so at all. Because of this and the high cost of shipping freight, the mission was open intermittently until 1932 when a government school was started. At that point people from Mansfield and Ketchumstuk began to settle around the mission on a relatively permanent basis. By the beginning of World War II, those people who had not previously moved to the village did so, and in 1942, the Tanacross Indian Reorganization Act (IRA) Council was chartered (Marcotte 1991).

In the early 1970s, to alleviate problems caused by flooding, the state of Alaska offered Tanacross residents the choice of moving across the river closer to the Alaska Highway or back to the village of Mansfield (or Dih thaad). They decided to move across the river. Since Mansfield is considered the spiritual home of the Tanacross people, the prospect of moving back was enticing. Many of the elders grew up there and practiced the hunting way of life that is the backbone of

Tanacross tradition. However, the state had agreed to provide road access, a school, and houses. A new road would open the area to non-Natives, with attendant friction over hunting and fishing rights. More important, Tanacross people wanted to preserve Mansfield as their refuge from the non-Native world. It is the one place where, uncharacteristically, people do not welcome strangers or uninvited guests.

The new village of Tanacross is situated at the end of a gravel road approximately one mile from the Alaska Highway. The 1990 population of the village was 106 (Alaska Department of Labor 1991). There are thirty-five occupied houses in the village arranged in neat lines along a series of gravel streets. In the center of the village are the community hall, where potlatches and bingo games are held, a post office, a log church, and a combination workshop/garage, which houses the village fire truck. Other public buildings include a school and gymnasium, a building housing a clinic, and the offices of the village corporation and council. Across the street from these is the village pump house and laundromat.

Most of the houses were built in the mid-1970s when the people moved from the old village and were financed through several development grants allocated by state and federal agencies and the regional nonprofit organization, the Tanana Chiefs Conference. These houses are of frame construction and have running water and electricity. Initially, all were provided with oil furnaces, but these proved too inefficient. Now every house has a wood stove as its primary source of heat. Within the last several years, a number of small log houses have been built to accommodate young men and women who have moved out of their parents' homes to set up independent households. None of these has facilities, but there are plans to install electricity and water. In addition, five houses have been built by private individuals, including this writer.

Cars, pickup trucks, and bicycles are parked in the front of many houses. Around the back and in the side yards one can catch a glimpse of dogs lounging on their houses, steam baths, wood yards, frames for tanning moose skins, boats, outboard motors, old cars, and snow machines. Many of the homes have caches in which are stored rifles, chainsaws, moose meat, untanned skins, and potlatch gifts that have been accumulated over the years. These stored gifts are an aspect of traditional wealth that can either be used as donations to another person's potlatch or given away at one's own potlatch.

THE SEASONS

Life in Tanacross follows a seasonal pattern. The busiest time of year is late summer and early fall when people prepare for the approaching winter. Gathering berries and hunting are two important activities. Women pick most of the berries (although a few men do join in) beginning in late July and continuing until sometime in September, depending on the weather. Berries are frozen or made into jams. Of all big game, moose are the most important (Marcotte 1991). Most men and boys—and a few women—hunt moose primarily at the end of August and the beginning of September when the season opens, although people do hunt moose at other times of the year, particularly in the event of a potlatch. Practically the entire moose is used, and the meat is frozen or cut into strips that are dried.

In the 1970s, almost all fall moose hunts were conducted along the Tanana River. The common practice was to go upriver early in the morning or early in the evening in a motorboat and float downstream to the village. In this way hunters hoped to catch moose in convenient locations as they walked along the bank or crossed the river. Another method required the hunter to sit on a hill overlooking the dry lakebeds that dot the landscape. If he saw a moose walking in the open, he watched until he was certain of the moose's route of travel; then he hurried to intercept the animal.

In 1987, while I was doing fieldwork, people still hunted on the river but more frequently along the Alaska Highway. This change was, in part, a result of the state of Alaska opening homesites in areas along the Tanana River. While only two or three cabins had been built, Tanacross people felt uncomfortable about hunting in what someone called "other people's backyard." But another reason for hunting along the road was the unusual presence of a herd of caribou that, as it moved along the edge of the mountains, came close to the highway on several occasions.

An important winter activity that follows the hunting season is trapping. The number of men who trap depends on the price of fur as well as the availability of serviceable snow machines. In 1987, five men trapped, but only two of them did so on a consistent basis. Traps are usually checked every two or three days, depending on the weather and if the snow machine is running. Since most of the traplines overlap, men occasionally check each other's traps. No one has a trapline that requires him to stay away from the village overnight, although people will travel up to seventy miles one way to check their traps. Most trappers check their sets alone, but occasionally two or three men will go together. During the winter of 1987, marten and lynx were the two most lucrative furs. People went out of their way to avoid trapping fox because it was considered "too cheap." In addition to the traplines, a number of men and women have snares set out in the woods around the village to catch hares, which are an important source of fresh meat during the winter.

Firewood is the most constant winter concern and can be secured by buying it or cutting it oneself. The Tanana Chiefs Conference has an energy assistance program in which people below a certain income level receive money to purchase fuel. A number of Tanacross people, especially elders and single women, use this program to buy wood from vendors in Tok. Those who cut their own wood go out of the village to stands of white spruce located close to the river.

During the dark months of November, December, and January, the Thanksgiving and Christmas holidays are focal points around which the community draws together to celebrate. At Thanksgiving the village hosts a big feast to which people from other villages are invited. On Christmas Eve there is often a school play in the community hall, a midnight church service, and a stroll around the village, during which participants stop at each house and sing Christmas carols in the Tanacross language and in English. On the following afternoon the whole village puts on a feast, after which gifts are distributed by Santa Claus and his helper.

The first months of the new year are usually the coldest as the heavy cold air slides into the valley bottoms producing inversions that push the temperature down to $-60°$ and $-70°F.$ for weeks at a time. This intense cold keeps everyone close to the village except for going to work or school. From January until late March, life in the village is quiet. Then, during the last week of March, the village explodes into activity as people get ready to host the annual Tanacross dogsled race attended by participants and spectators from all over the state.

Dogsled racing could be considered the Alaska state sport, and it is an activity in which Native people excel and often dominate. The Tanacross race is run over a weekend. On the eve of the race there is a banquet, hosted by the village, and a drawing for race positions. On the following morning, the trails are groomed and barriers erected to guide the racers along the village streets. A public address system is also installed. The race itself is run during the middle of the afternoon, the participants racing along a network of trails surrounding the village. Because dogsled racing is essentially a spectator sport, most of the spectators spend their time socializing, eating, and purchasing raffle tickets for prizes such as a hand-tanned moose skin, a .30-.30 Winchester rifle, or a dinner at a restaurant in Tok.

After the race, the village settles back to wait for spring breakup. By mid-April, the days are noticeably longer and much warmer. May is the month for school trips, usually to Seattle, but students have also gone to Los Angeles and as far away as Japan. Those who have regular seasonal employment begin work in May. In late May and early June, the fire-fighting season begins.

The major subsistence activity of the summer is fishing, which is done during June, July, and early August. As noted above, several kinds of fish are caught, but whitefish is by far the most favored species (Marcotte 1991: 165). All whitefish are caught in the clear waters of Mansfield Creek using a dip net set into a weir. Once caught, the fish are split and air dried. A variety of fish are also caught in the Tanana River using a gill net, but this method is not especially effective. Although salmon are occasionally caught in the Tanana, the major source is the Copper River. In late June and July, Tanacross people go to the Ahtna villages of Gulkana and

Copper Center and rent fish wheels from friends and relatives to catch their salmon.

EMPLOYMENT

Stable employment is scarce in Tanacross. Out of a population of sixty-nine adults, only five were employed during each of the preceding twelve months of 1987 (Marcotte 1991: 35). During that same period the average annual income was $14,106. Almost one-fourth of the jobs available required people to work outside the region, and these jobs lasted on average only six weeks or less (ibid., 87).

Employment opportunities in the community include work as teacher's aide, school custodian, part-time postmaster, full-time alcoholism counselor, and community health aide, who is trained to treat emergencies and dispense medicine. Outside the community two or three people are employed on a full-time basis by the Tanana Chiefs Conference, a nonprofit organization founded under the Alaska Native Claims Settlement Act (ANCSA), which has a subregional office in Tok. Other employment found outside the community is related to the oil industry. At one point in 1987, four Tanacross people worked on the North Slope, three as roughnecks on oil rigs run by Doyon Ltd. and one as a housekeeper maintaining the living quarters. The work cycle was two weeks on and two weeks off.

Additional employment found outside the community is seasonal work for the state of Alaska in highway maintenance, state campground maintenance, and forest fire suppression. These, along with work in the construction industry, are relatively well paying. The most common employment is fighting forest fires. During the summer of

1987, the village fielded two sixteen-person crews (male and female) composed of Tanacross residents and a number of non-Native people from Tok. These crews worked only during emergencies. During the 1987 season, they worked sporadically in Alaska until late summer, when they were called to fight fires in northern California for about three weeks. Since 1987, the state of Alaska and the federal government have changed their policy on fire suppression: many fires are now allowed to burn, except if they threaten human life or property. As a consequence, firefighting is not as lucrative as it once was.

SOCIAL ORGANIZATION

Tanacross is characterized by a single network of kin ties and marriage alliances that encompasses every permanent resident. Within this network there are four basic units of social interaction: household, extended family, village, and sib. The primary economic and social unit is the household. Members of the household eat together, sleep under the same roof, and share whatever resources each member earns or receives. There are thirty-five permanent households in the village varying in size from a single person to families that include three generations. The majority of households are composed of married couples with children.

Next in size and importance is the extended family. Because kin ties extend to so many people, the entire village could be considered an extended family. In this instance I define the extended family as a set of parents, their children, the children's spouses, and grandchildren. While members periodically share food, particularly on special occasions such as birthdays, they do not usually live under the same roof. The extended family is the basis for initiating social and political action within the village, and individuals can usually rely on siblings or grown children for support. Sometimes this leads to a situation in which one family dominates the planning of village social activities. As a matter of course, this seemingly aggressive behavior is roundly criticized.

The village as a unit may be defined as the sum total of the population. Native people, however, often restrict the definition to those people who are descended from the people who lived in Mansfield or Ketchumstuk. A person who marries into the village but whose ancestors come from another village is not considered to be from Tanacross. However it is defined, the village is the principal reference for the young people; people under the age of thirty have little idea of the sib structure. Today the village often acts together to put on feasts and potlatches, and it has a baseball team and a Native dance ensemble. Although the basis of the young people's identity has shifted from the sib to the village, the elders as well as some who are middle-aged, continue to see the importance of the sib. For them, it is the guiding principal in the distribution of goods during the potlatch.

Traditional Athapaskan society in east-central Alaska is divided into exogamous moieties that "function primarily in dividing individuals into 'opposites' who intermarry, help each other at life crises, particularly at death, and who entertain each other at potlatches" (de Laguna 1975: 89–90). Each moiety consists of a number of sibs (Murdock 1960: 47) or consanguineous groups based on matrilineal descent and identified by name. Reciprocal obligations between opposing sibs are the focus of exchange in the potlatch, and success or failure at carrying out these responsibilities reflects the social status of individuals, families, and sibs.

Theoretically, the sib is composed of all its members scattered among Alaskan and Canadian Natives, and the same sibs found in Tanacross are also found among other Athapaskan groups (de Laguna 1975).[1] In actual practice, however, the sib is composed of those people who know each other and who live in the Upper Tanana Region (Guedon 1974: 95). At the village level, Marie-Françoise Guedon (ibid., 95) identifies the "localized sib" or "lineage," as she sometimes calls it, which consists of members of the same sib who form a smaller but better integrated unit (ibid.). In Tanacross there are two dominant localized sibs, the Dikagiyu and the Naltsiin/'Al si' dEndi', which are considered opposites and whose members are considered suitable marriage partners. A third sib, the Tc'a·z, has few members and is considered a "relative" of the Dikagiyu. While members of the Dikagiyu and the Naltsiin/'Al si' dEndi' sibs are supposed to marry, today few young people succumb to their elders' pressure about whom to marry. In the village there are approximately thirty-two Naltsiin/'Al si' dEndi', thirty-two Dikagiyu, and sixteen Tc'a·z.

It should be understood that the social organization is fluid as the sib structure is constantly restructured to meet local exigencies (de Laguna 1975). Some people, for example, separate the Naltsiin and 'Al si' dEndi', while others say they are practically one and the same and that 'Al si' dEndi' is the potlatch name for the sib. This fluidity is further exemplified in Tetlin (Guedon 1974), where the Dikagiyu, Naltsiin, and 'Al si' dEndi' are considered to be in the same "Naltsina" moiety while the Tc'a·z or "Tc'iaaz" are placed in the opposite moiety. Also, the 'Al si' dEndi' are considered unique among the Ahtna because they allow intramoiety marriage (Kari 1986: 47). Although each of these sibs is found throughout most of interior Alaska (see n. 1), in Tanacross the Tc'a·z are said to have come from down the Tanana River, and there is a large hill called Ch'inchedL Teyy', which stands for a leader of the Tc'a·z sib. The Naltsiin and 'Al si' dEndi' sibs are also considered to have come from such places as the village of Ketchumstuk and down the Tanana River. Only the Dikagiyu and possibly the Tc'I'tcElyu sibs are considered indigenous to the immediate area.

CHAPTER 2

Invasion

Traders, Missionaries, and Government Men in the Upper Tanana

Traders, missionaries, and government men had one aim, to change Native people. Although sharing this goal, traders and missionaries followed different agendas. Traders were interested in drawing Native people into capitalist relationships, while missionaries worked to create Christian Native communities isolated from what they perceived to be the worst influences of American society, namely, lower-class elements out to exploit Native people. The government's agenda was to keep the peace, facilitate development, and create model citizens. Before World War II, this agenda was filtered through local traders and missionaries who acted as government agents. In this chapter I outline the changes that have occurred in Tanacross culture through contact with these groups. The changes desired by these outside interests were not, however, simply imposed on the Tanacross people; they were mutually determined through the interplay of external forces with the internal dynamics of Athapaskan society.

THE PROTOCONTACT PERIOD: 1780–1867

The first European trade goods to reach the upper Tanana River may have come in the late seventeenth or early eighteenth century through Russian traders in Siberia who were actively trading with the Chukchi (VanStone 1979: 63). In turn, the Chukchi traded with the Inupiat at annual trade fairs on the west coast of Alaska. These fairs were also attended by Athapaskans from the Koyukuk River who had trade connections with other Athapaskans in the interior (Zagoskin 1967: 152). The Inupiat also made expeditions to the Yukon River, to trade with the Ingalik Athapaskans, or Deg hit'an, living on the lower middle Yukon and Innoko rivers (VanStone 1979: 64). From the Koyukon and Deg hit'an, the trade moved inland via the Yukon, Kuskokwim, and Tanana rivers. This easterly movement of goods was accompanied by a westerly flow of goods channeled along indigenous networks linking the interior of Alaska with the Northwest Coast and Canada. In the late eighteenth century, Russian and British trading companies tied into these Native networks by establishing posts in southwestern Alaska and western Canada.[1]

During the 1780s, two competing Russian companies began trading into the interior of Alaska through posts located initially on Kodiak Island and later at Cook Inlet and Prince William Sound. In 1799, the competition ended when the Russian American Company received an Imperial charter granting it a monopoly over all of Alaska. By 1840, the company had expanded operations by setting up a post near Taral on the middle Copper River (Ketz 1983: 25) and establishing redoubts, as they were called, on the middle Kuskokwim River, on St. Michael Island (VanStone 1979:

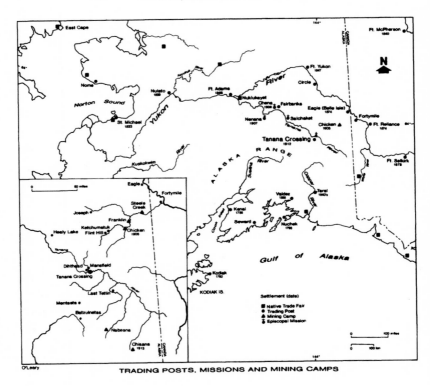

TRADING POSTS, MISSIONS AND MINING CAMPS

48–49), and at Nulato near the confluence of the Koyukuk and Yukon rivers (Zagoskin 1967: 146). This monopoly was directly challenged in 1847–48 by the establishment of two Hudson's Bay Company posts on the Yukon River: Fort Selkirk and Fort Yukon. Consequently, by 1850, the Native people on the upper Tanana River were surrounded by trading companies that had yet to penetrate their territory.

Prior to 1850, trade goods reached the upper Tanana River through a variety of intermediaries, such as the Ahtna,

Tutchone, and Han (McKennan 1959).[2] These groups had access to goods that came directly from Russian or English traders or through other Native groups. The Ahtna, for example, had direct access to goods from Russian posts located on Cook Inlet, the lower Copper River, and Prince William Sound (de Laguna and McClellan 1981: 650–51; Ketz 1983), while the Southern Tutchone received goods from the Chilkat Tlingit who traded with American and English ships plying the waters off the Northwest Coast (McClellan 1975). The Han people living north of the Tanana on the Yukon River traded at Hudson's Bay Company posts in western Canada and at Fort Yukon (Murray 1910: 51). Upper Tanana traders met these intermediaries at various locations. The Tutchone, for instance, were met at an annual rendezvous on the White River near the present international boundary (McKennan 1959: 129) and near the mouth of the Klondike River, while the Ahtna may have been met at various locations in their own country. Trade revolved around a variety of indigenous products and European trade goods. Interior Athapaskans exchanged tanned caribou and moose skins, native copper, furs, and tailored clothing with the coastal Tlingit for dentalium shells, Chilkat dance blankets, medicinal roots, and fish grease, in addition to such manufactured items as pipes, beads, knives, mirrors, leaf tobacco, and tea (McClellan 1964: 7, 1975: 505).[3]

THE EARLY CONTACT PERIOD: 1867–1912

There is no record of exactly when Tanacross people began trading directly with Europeans. First encounters may have occurred in the 1840s at an annual rendezvous called Nuklukayet at the confluence of the Yukon and Tanana rivers.

Koyukon, Gwich'in, and Tanana River people gathered there to socialize and trade with each other, with Russians from Nulato, and with Hudson's Bay Company employees from Fort Yukon. It is possible that Tanacross and Upper Tanana people visited the Hudson's Bay Company posts at Fort Yukon and Fort Selkirk, but there is no evidence for this.[4] Although William Healy Dall (1870: 108) indicates that Tanana River Natives visited Fort Yukon, there is no evidence these were Tanacross or Upper Tanana people. Certainly by the 1870s, people from the Upper Tanana Region made annual trips to Nuklukayet station or Fort Adams, established in 1868 by the Pioneer Company (McKennan 1981: 566–67; Mercier 1986).

The Pioneer Company moved into Alaska after the territory was purchased by the United States in 1867. At this point the development of interior Alaska trade increased sharply as a number of competing firms stretched up the Yukon, establishing posts along the river as far as the mouth of the Klondike River in western Yukon Territory. According to one chief trader, François Mercier, the initial impetus for building posts on the upper Yukon was to open unexploited areas and enhance trade relations with the remote upper Yukon and upper Tanana River people (Mercier 1986: 1–2). Before this, Native American trappers had been obliged to take their furs either to Fort Yukon or Nuklukayet or trade with Tutchone middlemen. But the establishment of Fort Reliance in 1874 and Belle Isle in 1880 on the upper Yukon brought the source of goods close to the boundary of Tanacross and Upper Tanana territory. Consequently, by the early 1880s, these people were making regular trading excursions to the Yukon (Allen 1887: 76, 80). This situation was only slightly altered with the discovery of gold on the Stewart and Fortymile rivers in 1886. Subsequently, the interest of the trading companies shifted to accommodate the needs of prospectors, and in 1887, two entrepreneurs, Leroy Napoleon McQuesten and Arthur Harper, established a post at the mouth of the Fortymile River to be closer to the placer mines (Mercier 1986: 3).

The discovery of gold on the Fortymile lured prospectors directly into Tanacross territory. Mining activities began in 1886 on Franklin Creek, a tributary of the Fortymile, and shortly thereafter on Chicken Creek, approximately twenty miles from the village of Ketchumstuk. Both mining camps were frequently visited by Tanacross and Upper Tanana people for "trade and diversion" (McKennan 1981: 567). In addition to the trading opportunities offered at Franklin and Chicken creeks, the Alaska Commercial Company opened a store at Steel Creek that, for a time, became a principal commercial center for the Tanacross people. Both the mining camps and the store at Steel Creek offered employment for a few Native men who worked on and off during the summer.

As a result, by 1890, the trading situation had altered considerably for the Tanacross people. No longer isolated from direct trade by geography or intermediaries, they became accustomed to a variety of foreign goods, including commercially made clothing, blankets, firearms, tobacco, beads, Tlingit button blankets, and dentalium shells (Allen 1887: 75, 132). In 1899, a government agent, C. E. Griffith, described an encounter with the people of Mansfield that displayed their increasing familiarity with Euro-Americans.

> These Indians were very friendly, and wanted to buy tobacco before anything else. They would, however, buy tea, sugar, guns and ammunition. They all seemed to be supplied with money and offered big prices for everything they wanted. They were intelligent, and all the young men spoke good English. (1900: 726)

THE MISSION AND TANANA RIVER TRADE: 1912–1940

The more recent phase of contact between American Natives and non-Natives is marked by the discovery of gold on the Chisana, a tributary of the Tanana River, the creation of the Episcopal mission, and the establishment of trading posts on the upper Tanana River. In 1913, gold was discovered on the Chisana River, which attracted thousands of people. During the winter of that year, miners killed an estimated two thousand mountain sheep and an undetermined number of caribou, forcing one band of Upper Tanana people to restructure their seasonal round (Capps 1916: 21). The presence of miners also attracted a variety of commercial establishments, including a cafe and saloon, giving Native people an opportunity to become familiar with foreign ways. In the sympathetic eyes of Archdeacon Hudson Stuck of the Protestant Episcopal Church, the presence of the miners resulted in the total degradation of the Native people.

It seems altogether impossible that a tribe of Indians should live in the near neighborhood of a considerable town without suffering degradation. There are always white men eager to associate with them to debauch the women and make a profit of the men; insensibly the native virtues are sapped, the simple native customs undergo sophistication into a grinning imitation of white customs; jaunty cast-off millinery displaces the decent handkerchief on the woman's head . . . [and] the men grow shiftless and casual picking up odd jobs around town and disdaining the hunting and fishing by which they used to live. (1917: 56–57)

Stuck believed "that he who would see the Indians at their best must see them remote from the settlements of the white men" (ibid., 57). The self-appointed counteragent to this demoralization of the Natives was Stuck's own Church. The basic problem facing Native Americans, as the Church saw it, was their very survival and the need to adapt to changing circumstances (Stuck 1917: 64). In his annual report to the contributors "outside," Peter Trimble Rowe, bishop of Alaska, wrote that "though they [the Natives] are the original possessors of the country, yet it is no longer theirs. They are driven back, their hunting grounds overrun and exhausted by the White man, and to get enough food for themselves and children is getting impossible. While subjects of laws they have no voice in, yet no laws seem to protect them" (Rowe 1910–11: 67–68). In essence, the Church viewed the Native people as victims of a system in which they were both morally and physically exploited by what the missionaries called "white men of the lower class" or "saloon element" (ibid., 68).

Certainly there is an element of class antagonism here. As a bastion of the Protestant middle class, the Episcopal Church saw the Native people as noble savages who had to be saved from the worst elements in Euro-American society. Equally important, Native people had to be saved from their own base instincts, which induced them to leave the forest and mimic non-Natives. Although the Church was paternalistic in its attitude, it reacted with a very real concern for the welfare of Native people, which must have been evident because they welcomed the establishment of a mission in their midst.

To avoid their further degradation, the Church sought to maintain Native American people in "regions of refuge" by advocating Native subsistence rights and building a series of mission stations at strategic points along the Yukon and Tanana rivers. On the Tanana, the first station was established in 1907 at Nenana, the second in 1908 at Chena, the third in 1909 at Salchaket village, and the fourth in 1912 at Tanana Crossing (McKennan 1981: 567).

By 1912, many Native people on the upper Tanana River had not seen or been acquainted with non-Natives, or so the missionaries believed. For this reason, the Church envisioned the Upper Tanana Region as fertile ground for the development of a pristine Christian Native community. As Bishop Rowe (1910–11: 68) commented, the Natives of this area "have not been hurt by the evil white element." "Naturally this means," wrote another missionary, "that in a place like Tanana Crossing where there is very little counteracting influence, we hold an unique position and have an excellent chance to remake the community." He went on to say, "Our village and the mission is the cause and the centralizing force" (Drane 1918: 190).

According to the Reverend E. A. McIntosh (1941: 3), who served at Tanana Crossing at various intervals between 1915 and 1941, the Church was induced to start a mission at Tanana Crossing by Chief Isaac, a headman of the Mansfield-Ketchumstuk people who "realized" the need for a mission in the area and "requested" the Church to build one. Subsequently, the Church purchased the buildings of an abandoned government telegraph station at the ford in the Tanana River called Tanana Crossing, and in the fall of 1912 Margaret Graves and Celia Wright, the first two missionaries, arrived.

From the start, the missionaries singled out the potlatch as a problem. Writing from Tanana Crossing in the winter of 1912, Graves (1913: 74) expressed the opinion that "most of the Indians are industrious; if they were less wasteful and could be made to abolish the potlatch system among themselves, I believe there would be very little real need." McIntosh, the third missionary to serve at Tanana Crossing, attempted to attract the Natives away from what he called their foolish superstitions,[5] including the potlatch, and keep out the "evil elements" and "remake the community" (Drane 1918: 190). This tactic was apparently unsuccessful, as McIntosh soon complained that "there will be the same ceremonies for God knows how long." Reluctantly he agreed "not to interfere with their old customs" [the potlatch] because he had been specifically asked by the Natives not to.[6] However, this hands-off policy did not continue.

In 1924, Arthur Wright, the missionary who replaced McIntosh at Tanacross, succeeded in convincing the village council to forbid extending or accepting "invitations for potlatching during the eight busy months of the year, i.e. October 1 to June 1" (Wright 1925: 18). According to Wright, the Natives were dependent on the mission, and the potlatch was an economic hardship that, as long as it continued, would inhibit the mission from making "the Indians respectable self-supporting people in this section of the country" (ibid., 20). After a year, Wright felt he was successful and wrote that the "abolition of potlatches at Tanacross has been going on a year . . . though the Indians did have potlatches in June and July" (ibid., 19).

Apparently this success was short-lived, because in the 1930s, John Hajdukovich renewed attempts to have the ceremony abolished. A trader and U.S. commissioner, Hajdukovich had considerable influence in the Upper Tanana Region. He had, for example, in 1930 been able to insist, much to the annoyance of the participants, that a potlatch, attended by the anthropologist Robert McKennan, end after only two days (McKennan 1959: 136). Hajdukovich thought the ritual had changed in sentiment and "developed into elaborate and expensive ceremony" that "required great personal sacrifice, which may mean perhaps an individual's entire earnings of a whole season" (Endicott 1928: 95). To control this extravagance, Hajdukovich had earlier urged the Bureau of Indian Affairs (BIA) to create reservations for the Native American people. In justifying his proposal, he explained that reservations would enable the government to control "the custom called the 'Potlatch' which costs the Indians yearly from ten to fifteen thousand dollars" and forces them to "deprive their women and children of food and clothing in order to save up for the Potlatch."[7] Subsequently, in 1930, President Herbert Hoover signed an executive order that established the 768,000-acre Tetlin reserve (Case 1984: 97).[8] Neither Hajdukovich nor the Church succeeded in abolishing the potlatch. In fact, the institution flourished (McKennan 1959: 135) and was continually elaborated and expanded during the pre–World War II period with trade goods received from entrepreneurs like Hajdukovich.

The establishment of the mission in 1912 and the discovery of gold on the Chisana River the following year stimulated the development of commercial navigation along the Tanana River (Cole 1979) and encouraged several traders to set up business in the region. The first permanent trader on the upper Tanana River was W. H. Newton, who opened a store at Healy River in 1907. In 1912, Newton moved part of his operation to Tanana Crossing and established caches both at Tetlin and at the mouth of the Nabesna River. In 1914, he sold out to John Strelic and went back to Healy River (McKennan 1959: 25; Cook 1989: 112). In 1924, a trader named Flannagin built a store near Tetlin. The Natives took advantage of this proliferation of posts by trading wherever they could get the best price for their fur, either going downriver to trade at Newton's store at Tanana Crossing or the mining camp at

Chicken Creek, where stocks of goods were more plentiful. The missionaries believed that Strelic was cheating the Natives (Drane 1918). McIntosh, for example, began trading with his congregation, which angered the professional traders. The resulting antagonism lasted for years, as missionaries and traders maneuvered to gain influence over the Native people.

By 1929, commercial operations had come to focus on four rival traders: Ted Lowell; Milo and John Hajdukovich, who had operations at Tanana Crossing, Tetlin, and the mouth of the Nabesna River; and Herman Kessler, who operated a business farther upriver and traded with the Scotty Creek band living adjacent to the Canada–U.S. border. Trade goods were brought in by boat during the summer months and cached at the various sites. In winter, the traders, traveling by dog team, met the Natives at various intervals during the trapping season. According to McKennan (1959: 26), they occasionally visited the Native people in their winter camps, but more often the Natives came to the traders' caches.

As the decades wore on to the outbreak of World War II, the Native people enjoyed a relative abundance and diversity of trade goods. By 1930, they had a choice of twenty-three different kinds of food offered by the traders at Tetlin and Tanana Crossing, including sugar, milk, butter, lard, rice, bacon, fresh eggs, carrots, beets, cabbage, and corn as well as dried apples, apricots, prunes, and peaches. There were clothes: wool shirts, wool coats, pants, rubber shoes, and socks. There were also a variety of household items: candles, pots and pans, dishes, phonographs, and records. There were also blankets: black ones for $14 each, creamy ones with green, brown, and yellow borders for $13.50 each. The traders sold rifles, .30-.30s and .22s, and bullets at $4.50 a box for the .30-.30s. Although repeating Henry rifles had been available from the trading station at Fortymile in the 1880s, smoothbore muzzle-loading guns were the arms of choice up until about 1914–15 when rifle ammunition became more readily available from the local traders.[9]

Trapping and Wage Labor

To acquire trade goods, Native people trapped, occasionally worked for the traders or some other enterprise, and sold handicrafts. Trapping was the most important activity, and during the winter the men spent long hours trapping lynx, marten, fox, and beaver. In the spring both men and women trapped and hunted muskrat. The price of furs and the size and value of the fur catch fluctuated from year to year, reflecting changes in the world market. In 1920, for instance, a red fox pelt was worth $80; in 1923, it was worth between $80 and $90, while a cross fox pelt was worth $100. But in 1928, the price of a red fox pelt dipped to $25, rebounding to $65 in 1929 (Strong 1972: chap. 5:49). The fluctuation in fur catches is reflected in the numbers of total exports. In 1920, the total exports of furs from Alaska was 200,000; it was 600,000 in 1940 (Melchoir 1987: 1122). I have no systematic data on the worth of the regional fur catch, but during the trapping season of 1929–30, it was estimated that the catch was worth between $20,000 and $25,000, down from the $40,000 to $50,000 of previous years (Back 1930: 31). Apparently a good portion of the catch was muskrat fur (Melchoir 1987: 1121).

Furs caught during the winter were traded in March, payment being made in goods, not cash (McKennan 1959: 26). Between then and November, people had no money, only the supplies they had traded for. As a result, some men tried to work during the summer to buy shells and "a few groceries." In Tanana Crossing it appears some men worked regularly for the traders, in particular, piloting the riverboats, which took great skill. Others worked only occasionally, when there was some immediate need for labor on large projects such as the construction of the airfield at Tanana Crossing or the school at Tetlin in the early 1930s.

A number of men whom I interviewed recalled their first working experience. One said that he earned his first wages in 1928, when he was twenty-four years old, cutting cordwood for the trader Flannagin at $2.50 a day. Later he ran a riverboat for Kessler and John Hajdukovich on a regular basis. Another man said that in 1933, when he was twenty-one, he worked for the first time for $5.50 a day clearing the airfield at Tanacross. The following summer, he worked at Tetlin on the new school until September, when he went back to Tanacross to work on the airfield again. This man also told me his father-in-law was attracted by the wages offered for work on the airfield. One summer day, the father-in-law left his family at its summer camp to travel the fifty miles back to Tanacross to buy groceries. He was gone nine days. Finally, fearing the worst, his son-in-law went to look for him and found him working. It should be noted that unlike most traders, who paid in commodities, and the missionaries, who expected the Natives to donate labor, these government projects paid cash.

During six days of August 1931, Titus Paul of Tanacross and Paul and John Healy of Healy Lake worked for Hajdukovich on his riverboat. They were paid in commodities as was the practice. For six days work, Titus received $30 worth of credit, $20 of which he spent on one box of tea, one box of .30-.30

shells, one dozen candles, and one heavy wool coat. Paul Healy bought socks, rubber shoes, and wool shirts.[10]

Other sources of income included working for big game guides and selling handicrafts. During the 1920s, several Tanacross men worked for Hajdukovich as assistant game guides taking wealthy hunters from the lower forty-eight states out to shoot caribou, Dall sheep, moose, and grizzly bear. Women sold beaded moccasins, which, in 1934—35, sold for $2 a pair, mittens, which sold for $4, and caribou skin socks, which sold for $.75 each. Snowshoes, sold by the men,[11] went for $4 and $5 a pair.[12] The Church, which encouraged the production of handicrafts, took, in lieu of cash for offerings, moccasins and mittens that were sent off to be sold in Fairbanks and New York.

Federal Intervention

Between 1920 and 1940, four forms of federal intervention occurred on the upper Tanana River. The first of these was the enactment of game laws, which are a major source of friction today. Second was the opening in Tanacross and Tetlin of federally subsidized schools. Third, a post office was opened in Tanacross and, along with the school, operated by the missionaries. Fourth was the building of an airfield across the river from the village.

Although trapping and wage labor had become a part of the Native economy, hunting, fishing, and gathering continued to be the primary sources of food, with caribou from the Fortymile herd being a major staple. Up until about 1905–10, communal caribou hunts, using drift fences and snares, had been the principal means of killing large numbers of caribou. This technique was phased out as ammunition for repeating rifles became readily available. With lever action rifles, hunting itself became more of an individual endeavor (Guedon 1974: 129) since a single hunter could harvest quantities of meat. However, the autumn caribou hunts continued to be a communal activity managed by the old leading men, who told people when to hunt and what animals to kill. As the time for the migration drew near, young men were dispatched into the hills to locate the herd. Once they found it, the whole village moved to intercept the migrating caribou. After the animals were killed, the meat was partially dried so that it could be easily packed back to Tanacross by people and dogs.

According to the naturalist O. J. Murie, who in 1921 made an extensive survey of the animal resources of the Upper Tanana Region, including the Fortymile caribou herd, Native hunters averaged 25 caribou each for the month of October, while some killed between 15 and 30 in two days. He also wrote that the people of Healy Lake were reported to have killed 51 moose in two and one-half months (possibly for a huge potlatch), and at a Tetlin potlatch in 1920, 22 moose were butchered and the skins given away as presents (Murie 1921).

Murie's attitude toward Native use of game was ambivalent. At one point he said that the "Indians were destructive to game" (Murie 1921), and on another occasion he declared that the "interior Indians along the Tanana River never seemed to waste wild meat; at the same time they are fond of unborn moose and caribou, and . . . each family kept too many dogs, feeding them perhaps as many as twenty-five caribou a summer" (Sherwood 1981: 172). Murie's comments were relayed to Washington, but whether they were instrumental in changing the game laws is unclear. Whatever the case, the fact is that by 1925 territorial game laws had been changed, ostensibly because non-Natives complained that Natives were abusing their privileges (ibid., 106).

The 1902 federal regulations pertaining to hunting in the territory of Alaska allowed Native people, along with miners and travelers, to kill game for food and clothing regardless of the season. The only restriction was that they could not sell or ship the meat. The federal game law of 1925 again classed Native people with miners and travelers, but it permitted no one to kill game out of season except when in "absolute need of food and other food is not available" (ibid.). Furthermore, this exemption could be revoked by the secretary of agriculture if he decided that game in a certain area was in danger of extermination. It appears that these laws were not immediately enforced among Native residents of the Upper Tanana Region, but they reinforced the principle that Native and non-Native hunters had equal rights to game, a standard that would have a tremendous impact in years to come.

The restructuring of game laws was only one indication of the expanding federal presence in the territory of Alaska. In 1931, the BIA appropriated $4,000 for a school at Tanana Crossing, and the Church offered the mission buildings as a facility. At this point, according to elders in Tanacross, many of the Mansfield-Ketchumstuk people decided to live permanently in the village at Tanana Crossing. The result was that families who had hunted and trapped together were often separated for extended periods during the winter months while the men were out on the traplines. The women stayed at home so the younger children could attend school. Along with the school, a post office was established which relied on deliveries by airplane in the winter and by riverboat in the summer. With the presence of the mission, the school, the post office, and the trading post, the village became the focal point of activity spatially reorienting the people away from outlying camps and villages, such as Ketchumstuk.

In the 1920s, the Alaska Road Commission was given the responsibility of constructing airfields throughout the territory. Under this mandate the commission opened a field at Tanana Crossing built with Alaska Native labor. In 1934, the field was upgraded to accommodate planes flying along a commercial route between Juneau, Fairbanks, and Nome (Haycox n.d.: 1), which the traders opposed because it enabled Native people to buy directly from mail order houses and to send out their furs.[13] Then, in August 1940, the airfield was designated part of the newly formed Northwest Staging Route, a secure airway linking the United States and Alaska (ibid.).

SUMMARY OF AN ERA: 1780–1940

The preceding history has been divided into three stages of contact. Stage one, the protocontact period (1780–1867), was characterized by the Tanacross people's irregular access to trade goods available initially through intermediaries and later through long-distance trips to the source of goods. The second stage, the early contact period (1867–1912), was noted for increasingly direct and regular trade through stations located close to the periphery of Tanacross territory. Such consistent access increased the Tanacross people's dependence on trade goods and drew them further into an economy based on the exchange of furs for goods. In the third stage, which I labeled the mission and Tanana River trade (1912–40), contact between Tanacross people and non-Natives was sustained through the direct presence of missionaries and traders in Tanacross territory. During this period, the Episcopal Church became an important influence in Tanacross culture, the federal government actively intervened, and people began working for wages.

The process of missionization, as Sergie Kan (1987b: 3) notes, should be viewed both as "a power struggle between Europeans and the natives" and "as a 'dialogue' between two different systems of meaning." Certainly, Native resistance to missionary attempts at abolishing the potlatch can be viewed as a struggle between two systems of meaning. Missionaries worked to instill in Native people what they thought were appropriate Protestant values of disciplined work, individual accumulation, and thrift so that Native people would become both "respectable" and "self-supporting." Native people, viewing the situation differently, continued the ostentatious and extravagant practice of the potlatch, though they attempted to accommodate the missionaries by holding the ceremony during the summer months only (Wright 1925: 19).

Yet even as Native people resisted missionary control over certain aspects of their lives, they internalized and reinterpreted Christian teachings on their own terms. Such a process is reflected in a story about a man named Big Mark. According to the story, Big Mark said that "Indians really think they are Christian and they really believe it. Inside people are really Christian, Jesus is part of good luck and if you live a long time hold Jesus responsible." His belief grew out of a particular experience he had when his wife was ill with tuberculosis and he was unable to hunt. He was "stuck" in Mansfield taking care of her. Eventually running out of money, they could not get flour to make bannock or rice. Depressed, Big Mark kneeled down to pray. The next day he shot a silver fox, which in those days was worth $500. Big Mark took his good fortune as a sign that God had graced him. He said the fox was sent by God because he never saw any sign, meaning he never saw any indication that the fox was there before he shot it.[14]

Such expressions of belief were often misinterpreted or denigrated by the missionaries, who alternately praised the Natives' apparent attachment to Christianity and complained about their ignorance of it. Arthur Wright, for instance, criticized the Indians for asking

> Why if God is as we say the father of us all, he does not provide for them filling their traps with fur animals and bring meat to their camp when they want it and ask for it, as their spirits do if properly involved. The idea of personal gain is the only idea with which they associate our Teaching of God.[15]

Big Mark's story and Wright's complaint illustrate a paradox in Native–non-Native relations. While the missionaries wanted the Natives to abandon the potlatch because it was wasteful and obstructed their economic independence, they thought it unseemly that Natives would pray for personal gain, even if they were starving.

Despite their attachment, Tanacross people feel ambivalent toward the modern church. They are greatly attached to the Episcopal Church's ideology and practice. Christian virtues of kindness, sharing, and love are equated with the virtues of traditional Native culture, the Indian way. Additionally, the Episcopal Church is esteemed as the church of the old people. To abandon it would be to abandon a traditional tie, and for this reason the dead are always buried with a Christian funeral service. At the same time, the public practice of Christianity is largely viewed as a non-Native domain, and Tanacross people believe they need a non-Native practitioner to correctly interpret Christian teachings. Further, while a minister from Tok serves the village, Tanacross people feel abandoned by the Church because it no longer provides a resident priest or supports a mission as it once did.

In economic terms, Tanacross people continued to live a relatively autonomous existence highly dependent on hunting, fishing, and trapping. Cast in a romantic light, this life appeared "rather independent and aristocratic" so that "when fur is scarce they must eat more caribou and dried fish and less of the White man's food sold by the traders" (Back 1930: 31). Closer to hard reality, the schoolteacher at Tanacross, Veta McIntosh, wrote in 1933 that children were absent from school not only because they were sick with chicken pox and the flu but also "because of a shortage of food. Fur being scarce most of the parents found it necessary to take their families with them and have the older ones assist in trapping and hunting. Older children were out hunting during the first spell of warm weather."[16] Yet despite these hardships, Native people produced enough surplus that they were able to channel it into the development and elaboration of the potlatch (McKennan 1959). Table 2 indicates the extent to which potlatching continued in the region prior to World War II. Note that the costs quoted for the two potlatches held in 1930 reflect 10 percent of the annual regional fur trade, which was reported to have been between $20,000 and $25,000.

A NEW ERA: WORLD WAR II AND THE ALASKA HIGHWAY

World War II and the construction of the Alaska Highway marked the beginning of a new era for the Tanacross people. While the highway was not the only factor in changing the old way of life, its consequences were substantially more disruptive than earlier contacts. The construction and use of the

Table 2
Historic Potlatches in the Upper Tanana and
Upper Copper River Areas, 1918–1930

Gifts	Cost of Ceremony	Year and Location	Source
200 blankets, undetermined amount of guns, pots and pans, skin coats, moccasins, mittens, cloth, and caribou meat	$4,000	1918 at Tanana Crossing	*Alaska Churchman*, Feb. 1918
An average of 50 to 80 blankets at a cost of $14 each and an average of 5 to 10 guns distributed at each potlatch; pots and pans and beadwork	Unknown	1923, 1925, 1926, 1927 at Tetlin and Batzulnetas	Field notes; Strong (1972)
Undetermined amount of blankets and guns, pots and pans, beadwork, cloth, moose meat, and store food	$15,000–$20,000	1927 at Healy Lake	Endicott (1928)
Guns, blankets, pots and pans, cloth used to eat on, Dall sheep meat, and store food	$2,000	1930 at Batzulnetas	McKennan (1959)
100 blankets, between 20 and 30 rifles, pots, beadwork, and cloth	$2,500	1930 at Mentasta	Back (1930)

road, which passed within two miles of the village, can be seen as a central thread in changes that began to take place after 1942. In his annual report of 1942, Bishop John Bentley of the Episcopal Church described the situation at Tanacross.

> The Rev. E. A. McIntosh is our priest-in-charge of St. Timothy's Mission. He and his people are living in a rapidly changing world. Until a few years ago, these people lived in a world to themselves, a world pretty much like the one their fathers and grandfathers had known. Their time was taken up entirely by hunting and fishing and trapping and the daily tasks that go to make up life in the wilderness. Today that whole primitive life has been shattered by the voice of the radio and the sound of airplane motors. Where rabbit and ptarmigan were hunted, there now stretches the long, hard surface of a splendid airport upon which land multi-motored planes on their way from Fairbanks to Juneau en route to the States. Also, the new international highway known as the Alcan Trail passes near the village site. These great new construction projects have afforded our people of the upper Tanana many varied jobs and have opened their eyes to a new civilization. Some of this has been good, and some of it has been of doubtful benefits to our people. However, no man is able to stay the course of empire, whether he would or not, and our people must learn to cope with the new world that has been thrust so suddenly upon them. (1943: 17)

Construction of a pioneer road began in March 1942, and the building of the permanent road was completed in October 1943. During the approximately seventeen months of construction, a total of 34,637 men came north to work on the highway (Cruikshank 1985: 175). One of the main construction camps was located at Tok and housed as many 5,000 personnel (Haycox n.d.: 4). After the war, in 1946, it was considered possibly the most modern, if not the most complete, maintenance center on the entire highway (ibid.).

The large influx of both military and civilian workers and the availability of jobs distorted the local hunting and trapping economy. Older outlying villages such as Healy Lake, Ketchumstuk, and Mansfield were abandoned as people seeking employment moved closer to the road. Men worked as guides for survey crews or as construction workers, while women served as domestic help or made money selling mittens, moccasins, and beadwork to the workers. Some Tanacross people believe that during the construction of the highway the Native economy involved approximately 50 percent wage labor. That is, while hunting was still considered the "regular life," almost everyone in the village devoted at least half of his or her time to earning cash for the purchase of food. A similar observation was made by some Ahtna people who live in the village of Mentasta: in the years "1942 to 1945 a switchover occurred in which over half of the diet of the native came from purchased groceries" (Strong 1972: chap. 6:3).

Although the war and road construction created a boom economy, it produced no lasting economic benefits for the majority of Native people. Furthermore, the road ended the isolation of the Upper Tanana Region so that after the war people could not simply return to the old seasonal round of hunting and trapping. Between 1939 and 1950, the non-Native population of Alaska doubled and the number of resident hunting licenses more than tripled, from about 9,000 in 1946 to 31,500 in 1955—56 (Sherwood 1981: 143). The road opened the region to many of these hunters, who came from Fairbanks and Anchorage. Increased hunting pressure brought more stringent government regulations.[17] As early as 1932, Ahtna people living around the highway settlement of

Copper Center had been imprisoned for game violations, and in 1947, a Native man from the Upper Ahtna village of Mentasta was jailed (Strong 1972: chap. 5:6). Although no Tanacross people were arrested, or ever have been, there was a growing antagonism to game wardens and game laws.

The Alaska Highway also affected Native demography and health. The presence of so many men from "outside" had an impact not only on Native and non-Native relations but also on male and female relations. Liaisons between Native women and soldiers produced children who were often left behind after the war, and some Native women who married soldiers left the region forever.

Although Tanacross people had been ravaged by epidemics of influenza, chicken pox, and pneumonia before the war, new epidemics accompanied the construction of the road. After 1940, outlying villages, such as Healy Lake, were struck by severe respiratory sickness and consequently abandoned as people moved to the nearby communities of Tanacross and Dot Lake (Cook 1989: 109). Tuberculosis was also epidemic, and alcohol became available on an unprecedented scale. Before the highway, liquor was rare in Tanacross or Upper Tanana villages. Elders remember today that before the war only one or two men drank, and alcohol was found predominantly in the mining camps on the Fortymile River. During the war, alcohol was easily obtained at the bars and liquor stores that opened in Tok. After the war, the road became a death trap for Native men who, after a night of drinking in Tok, tried to make it back to the village.

The views of Native leaders on problems created by the highway were related to Walter Goldschmidt, an anthropologist who visited the villages of Tetlin, Northway, and Tanacross in the summer of 1946. He wrote that

Native leaders are concerned over the encroachment of whites
into their historic domain. They are not hostile to whites as
individuals, nor to the now no longer strange ways of the
white man. They are, however, concerned with two effects of
this encroachment: the depletion of the fur animals from
which they get a large portion of their livelihood, and the
moral effects of liquor and other urban delights upon the
youth of the community and the resultant destruction of their
homogeneity which is so important to the economic welfare
of the entire group. (1946: 17)

These comments clearly state two of the major problems
that would confront Tanacross people in the remaining
decades of the twentieth century: threats to the land and
their autonomy and the debilitating effects of alcoholism
on the spirit.

AFTER WORLD WAR II:
THE ALASKA NATIVE CLAIMS SETTLEMENT ACT

At the end of World War II, the majority of Alaska Native
people lived in isolated communities away from urban centers.
Continued use of land their ancestors had occupied for centu-
ries seemed assured. But beginning in the late 1950s, this
right was threatened. One of the most serious threats came
from a provision in the Statehood Act of 1958 that authorized
the new state government to select and obtain title to 103
million acres of land in the public domain (Arnold 1976).
These selections were made without Native consultation and
frequently conflicted with Native claims, such as those made
by the Tanacross people.

On November 6, 1950, Tanacross petitioned the Department of Interior for a 63,000-acre reservation that would

include much of the traditional land used by the Tanacross people. No action was taken on the claim until 1961, when it was rejected. An appeal was never acted on, and some of the land was approved for state selection (Debo 1970: 402). In 1964, the state of Alaska offered some of the land claimed by Tanacross people as homesites, and in response, the village, under the leadership of Chief Andrew Isaac, filed a blanket claim to the whole area. One year later the state again offered the land, this time as "wilderness estates," which were advertised at the New York World's Fair. At this point the Native newspaper, the *Tundra Times*, published a series of articles about the Tanacross claim that brought to a halt the state's plans (ibid., 403).

Problems similar to those confronting Tanacross led Alaska Natives, in 1966, to form the Alaska Federation of Natives (AFN). The focus of the AFN was to halt state land selections until all Native claims were settled. In 1966, the AFN convinced the secretary of the interior, Stewart Udall, to impose a freeze on state selections. The crises was brought to a head in 1968 when oil was discovered on Alaska's North Slope and the state realized over $900 million from lease sales. Pressure for a settlement of Native claims became intense, but it was not until December 1971 that President Richard M. Nixon finally signed Public Law 93-203, the Alaska Native Claims Settlement Act (ANCSA).

Through the settlement Alaska Native people received 43.7 million acres of land and $962.5 million as compensation for the extinguishment of all aboriginal rights, including aboriginal hunting and fishing rights. Reiterated in ANCSA, however, was the "trust" responsibility of the federal government to protect Alaska Native people. Congress also declared that it expected the secretary of the interior and the state of

Alaska to provide for the "subsistence needs" of Alaska Natives (Case 1984: 294).

Under ANCSA, 13 regional and 224 village corporations were formed. Regional corporations were created with the clear intention of earning a profit with money and lands received in the settlement. Regional Native associations, which had existed before ANCSA, were incorporated as nonprofit organizations responsible for providing services to Native people in the areas of health, education, housing, and employment assistance. Village corporations had the choice of incorporating either on a profit or a nonprofit basis. Shareholders in both the regional and the village corporations were Native people born before December 1971. Each shareholder was issued 200 shares of stock: 100 shares from the regional corporation and 100 shares from his or her village corporation. Regional corporations were given the right to manage the subsurface rights of village corporation lands within their region as well as other corporation lands and funds received through the settlement. Village corporations were given the right to manage the surface rights of their land and money received through the settlement. Tanacross is now a member of Doyon Ltd., the regional profit corporation, and a member of the Tanana Chiefs Conference Incorporated, the regional nonprofit organization. The village also formed a profit-making corporation, Tanacross Incorporated.

At the time, ANCSA was considered unique because Native people were involved on an unprecedented scale. The assets provided by the settlement were viewed by many as a vehicle for economic development and the final assimilation of Native people into mainstream American society. There were problems, however. First, many Native people had no desire to be assimilated. ANCSA did not emanate from their

vision of society, which emphasizes kinship, reciprocal obligations, and communal ownership of property. Rather, it
arose out of the vision of the dominant society, which, as Tom
Moorehouse (1989: 197) states, is "one of a single Alaskan
community, under a state constitution expressing consensus
values of individualism, equal opportunity, private property
and economic development." Second, in its original form,
ANCSA restricted the sale of stock and protected regional
and village lands until 1991. After that, these exclusions
protecting land and Native control were to be removed and
the land could be lost through bankruptcy or taxes. Shares in
both village and regional corporations could also be sold on
the open market, threatening Native control. Furthermore,
Native people born after 1971 were not issued stock and were
therefore unable to actively participate in the corporations.

As problems with the law became apparent, pressure grew
within the Native community for Congress to amend the act,
which was done in 1987. The amendments provide automatic
protection of undeveloped corporate lands from taxation and
adverse possession or seizure for debt or bankruptcy. Also
restricted was the sale of stock to outsiders without the
approval of a majority of stockholders in any particular corporation. Finally, the amendments also provide for issuing new
stock to those born after 1971.

Although addressing failings in the law, the amendments
could not resolve the issue of aboriginal rights to hunting and
fishing. These rights had been "extinguished" by ANCSA,
but Congress still expected them to be protected by the state
of Alaska and the secretary of the interior. In the aftermath of
ANCSA, however, it became clear to Congress and the
Native people that too many legal, political, and economic
obstacles existed for either the state or Interior to adequately

protect Native interests (Case 1984: 296–97). In 1980, Congress passed the Alaska National Interest Lands Conservation Act (ANILCA) (P. L. 96-487). Title VIII of ANILCA was intended to carry out the subsistence-related policies and fulfill the purposes of ANCSA (ibid., 299). While subsistence rights were established for both Native and non-Native rural residents, it was clear, as David Case points out, that Title VIII was created to protect the "physical, economic, traditional and cultural existence of Alaska Native people" (ibid.).

Until 1989, the state complied with the federal mandate on subsistence and instituted a rural preference that provided that if stocks of fish and game declined within a region, the rural residents of that region were given priority over people from other parts of the state to harvest game. In 1989, the Alaska Supreme Court found the rural priority unconstitutional and prohibited the state from using residency as a basis of subsistence hunting and fishing. At this point the state was out of compliance with ANILCA, and the federal government took over management of game on federal lands (Caulfield 1992: 26).

ANCSA has produced varying results in the Upper Tanana Region. The act has provided some employment on the local level, but stable employment is still scarce and the people's standard of living has not been raised substantially. Local Native people have benefited from a statewide enhancement of Native political and economic power that has reduced the stigma attached to being Native. But ANCSA has not diminished tensions between Natives and non-Natives, who feel that Native people have been compensated more than enough for the loss of aboriginal rights and resent both what they see as free handouts to Native people and the economic and political power Native people wield because of the settlement.

A flashpoint for the tension between Natives and non-Natives is the subsistence issue. As Steve McNabb (1991: 70) observes, subsistence has become an idiom for Native culture, and any threat to subsistence is perceived as a threat to cultural identity. Tanacross people generally feel that anyone who is poor, regardless of his or her cultural background, should have subsistence rights. But they also feel that as Native people they should have rights that supersede any sport hunter, that is, anyone who has a regular income, which is thought to be the vast majority of non-Native people. There is also a growing feeling that Native people should be able to manage local game populations. As one young man said, "The Inupiat can manage whales, why can't we manage moose?"

The recent history of Tanacross is characterized by the long-term trend of the dominant society to move Alaska Natives toward mainstream political and economic institutions and behavior. Initially, religion and ideology were used to rationalize efforts to assimilate or absorb Alaska Natives. More recently, politics and bureaucracy have been the instruments, as evidenced in the statehood movement and implementation of ANCSA (Moorehouse 1989: 7). Yet Tanacross people have not simply succumbed; they have responded by accommodating when pressured to do so, resisting where possible, and integrating when they find it desirable. Through this process, they have created and re-created their culture. In the next chapter, we examine one aspect of the Native response, the transformation of trade goods into potlatch gifts.

CHAPTER 3

The Native Response
The Integration of Trade Goods into the Potlatch

As we have seen, the people of Tanacross accepted much of what the traders, missionaries, and government had to offer, but they refused to give up the potlatch and in doing so, resisted the basic, more profound changes sought by non-Natives. In effect, they resisted all that the traders and missionaries understood to be "natural," that is, personal accumulation, thrift, and investment. It is argued, nevertheless, that the use of trade goods changed the meaning and significance of the potlatch. McKennan (1959: 133), for example, thought that trade goods represented a contradiction between values based on egalitarianism and sharing and values based on the competitive distribution of wealth for prestige. He speculated that a succession of trade goods became symbolic of individual achievement, each being replaced by another at various historical intervals. The earliest objects of esteem, dentalium shells, were eventually replaced by beads introduced by the Hudson's Bay Company; these were eventually replaced by blankets and guns introduced through the American trade. It is clear, however, that far from disrupting the Athapaskan cultural system, trade goods were "indigenized" (Gualtieri 1980: 57), or given Native meanings reflecting both the indigenous cultural system and developing relations between Natives and non-Natives.

In historic Tanacross culture, the production, consumption, and distribution of things were elements of a totality and not autonomous spheres.[1] Within this totality, objects were not alienated from their social context but tied to people and relationships. The intimate connection between individuals and objects was reflected in the idea that objects can be invested with a spirit or personal essence.[2] In Tanacross culture, this spirit is found in everything.[3] For example, a bandolier of dentalium shells once owned by a spiritually powerful man was said to have the power to heal sickness and was hung over a patient's sickbed while another one of his belongings was placed under the pillow. Similarly, the host of a mortuary potlatch invested his emotions in the gifts, thereby objectifying his emotional pain. He then purged himself of sadness and grief by distributing the gifts to his guests so they too could share in his sorrow. Thus the host and guests were bound in a reciprocal relationship based on shared emotional pain. At the same time, the gifts are objects of intrinsic value that can be used by the guests for their material existence.[4]

In distributing objects, potlatch hosts gave a part of themselves, and they did so because they owed themselves and their possessions to others (Mauss 1967: 44). A host's place in history not only was predicated on his distributions but also emanated from the actions of his paternal and maternal ancestors. For this reason Tanacross people say that it is not the living host who gives the potlatch but his ancestors. The host's connections to the past and present are cemented through the distribution of gifts. By distributing guns, blankets, and beads to the assembled guests, the host demonstrates his relationship to and his feelings for his paternal relatives and potential affines. This is summed up in the statement "You were born because of your father's people, that is why you pay back" (Guedon 1981: 578). Through these distributions the host gains prestige as he symbolically ensures his guests' existence by giving them guns to hunt and blankets to keep them warm. In providing such gifts to possible marriage partners, the host also ensures the existence of succeeding generations.

The host demonstrates his respect for the maternal side by wearing dentalium shell necklaces, skin coats, and bandoliers of beads. Through these objects, which either literally or figuratively belonged to the ancestors, the host reflects their accomplishments, absorbs some of their power, and is enlarged beyond himself. This demonstration is considered *diichaagh*, "something really great," and earns the host prestige in the eyes of his maternal relatives. At the same time, the host establishes his social position in relation to that of his guests. Through this interplay between the quest for individual prestige and the maintenance of social relations, the potlatch host enhances his position.

The animate power of objects is also evident in the idea that potlatch gifts actively attract wealth. This is why a potlatch host keeps a small piece of blanket or why a young person who has made his first potlatch wears gloves. Wearing gloves is said to be "just like you tie it [the wealth] down." The spirit of the objects adhered to the gloves instead of being washed away when the host washed his hands. Like the piece of blanket, the gloves were kept so they could attract wealth and enhance the host's reputation as a person able to participate in and sustain relationships.

TRADE AND THE ROLE OF LEADING MEN

Distinctions in status always have existed in Tanacross culture, but the access to foreign goods, whether from Euro-American or indigenous sources, reinforced them. Whatever the circumstance, individual status was only enhanced through a person's ability to maintain his social relationships. As Tanacross people say, it was only by actively caring for his people that a leading man was able to garner prestige.

Leading men organized and controlled the trade during the protocontact (1780–1867) and early contact periods (1867–1912) through the distribution of goods. In the middle of the nineteenth century, they organized annual trips down the Tanana River to Nuklukayet and "hired" their nephews and other relatives as packers, paying them in ammunition, tea, or chewing tobacco at the end of the trip. It should be noted that "hiring" does not indicate a contractual agreement but rather a form of generalized reciprocity. An older woman from Dot Lake, who described the trading expeditions of her great-grandfather down the Tanana, said,

> [On the] first of June my grandpa go down, they go by canoe, bring all his nephew and all his uncle, all go down to Tanana. All people go together, bought all that shell, tea, chew, whatever they use, come back when berries ready to ripe, August or September. Hard trip, but old people pay so much a day for the packing. His own relative pack stuff for them, the leader old people take care. If chief hire you and [you] do it [work] for them they give you stuff, if you get hard up, they share with shell, tea and all that stuff. The chief keeps up all his people, just like one family. (Interview conducted February 1987)

The "grandpa" to whom she referred was a man called Tsiint-le' who was a nineteenth-century "rich man" or leader.

He and his brother (some say first cousin), Ket-laata', known as Kheeltat in the literature, were headmen for the Dikagiyu sib and important figures in Tanacross history. Both were purported to have been very rich—according to some, the richest men in the whole Upper Tanana Region. Today a majority of the Tanacross people claim descent from these two men. Their status came, in part, from their control over subsistence production and from wealth derived from trade conducted initially at Nuklukayet and later on the Yukon River at Fort Reliance, Belle Isle, and Fortymile. The trading ventures of Ket-laata' to the Yukon are documented by Lt. Henry T. Allen who, after a short visit with the chief at his village of Dih thaad, in the summer of 1885, wrote that Ket-laata' would meet him "on the upper Yukon in July, when the steamboat would have arrived" (Allen 1887: 80).

Allen alludes to the wealth of the Native people in the Upper Tanana Region: "Their clothing indicated more easy communication with a trading station than did that of the Atnatanas [Ahtna]; We realized from their appearance that better times awaited us" (ibid., 75). He goes on to say that the Natives' "frequency of visits" to the Yukon River had "considerable influence in modifying their customs and dress. They have almost entirely ceased to wear nose-rings, and but a few wear ornaments in their ears" (ibid., 136). He also mentions that muzzle-loading shotguns were displacing the bow and arrow (ibid., 132).

The importance of Tsiint-le' is suggested by a story in which he is said to have killed one or two young boys in a fit of temper during a potlatch (Paul 1974: 28). Ordinarily, such an offense might have ended in the death of the killer, but Tsiint-le' was spared because of his significance in trade. As the story relates, Tsiint-le' had a good friend in the village "where these people look[ed] for him" and this "man good friend[5]–not for love but for business, like trading." To protect Tsiint-le', his friend or "partner" put both arms around him "so he [wouldn't] be hurt too much" while "some other men beat him up but not to kill." Afterward the partner helped him up and "talk, talk to his people to get [Tsiint-le'] out of his trouble, just like lawyer!" Tsiint-le' told them, "I don't want no more trouble! I don't want no more strings on me, no more people follow me! Whoever have hard feelings with me, I pay. Tell me how much." For this, Tsiint-le' put on a big potlatch and paid "Big gifts!" to appease the deceased's relatives (ibid., 28–29).

This story illustrates two points about leadership. The leader is portrayed as pivotal in the management of trade (Allen 1887; Kari 1986), and he is seen as able to settle serious disputes through the distribution of gifts, which ensures the stability of social relations. In this case, the success of the leader was also based on his social position, for Tsiint-le' was also the leading man of the prominent Dikagiyu sib whose status is reflected in its recognized "ownership" of two highly valued objects: the dentalium shell and the gun.

THE GOODS: DENTALIUM SHELLS, BEADS, GUNS, AND BLANKETS

Dentalium shells derive from short, tusk-shaped mollusks found in the waters off the Northwest Coast. As symbols of wealth and prestige, they are highly valued by many Athapaskan groups both in Canada and Alaska. According to Tanacross and Upper Tanana oral tradition, the shells were first received as gifts from the Guu, or "Brush Indians." One story relates how the shells were acquired as a reward for saving a stranger from a bear attack.

A "man" sees that a Brush Man is being stalked by the bear. As the Brush Man attempts to flee the bear, his shirt becomes entangled in the brush and he falls. The bear is on top of him immediately, and the stranger attempts to stab the bear in the mouth with his knife. By this time the "man" arrives and spears the bear in the heart. He then clubs him. The bear dies, and the two men smile at each other. They then sit back to back, and the stranger tells the "man" that he should clear a tree of all its limbs so that he will be able to find this spot again. The stranger then says that the "man" should come back to this spot every year and take whatever he finds useful hanging from the tree. The next year the "man" finds "necklace beads" or dentalium shells hanging from the tree. (Recorded in Tanacross, August 1983)[6]

Some people say the man who saved the Brush Indian's life was a member of the Dikagiyu sib, and through his act, they were the first to acquire the shells. Consequently, they were considered to be "owners" of the shells and to be wealthy people as reflected in the statement "Dik'agiyu, they're millionaire tribe, high price people" (Guedon 1974: 69). Ownership in this sense did not indicate exclusive rights to the shells but meant that the Dikagiyu had to be always acknowledged as the first people to have the shell. Thus their status was continually reconfirmed.

During the fur trade, dentalium became symbolic of wealth obtained by leading men through their management and control of the trade. Unlike other types of property, the shells were not shared or redistributed (Strong 1972: chap. 5:30) but displayed as symbols of individual status and handed down from generation to generation. According to one person who was born on the Goodpaster River in the 1860s,

Wampum [dentalium] was money but people didn't hide it; they wore it. Just rich people and chiefs and their wives could

wear wampum in big wide collars around their necks and long
earrings hanging clear down to their shoulders and even
longer sometimes . . . [and] sometimes when there was a
potlatch, mama said the chief put on a neck-piece with beads
just solid and big, big breast plate all over beads and he was
beautiful. (Anderson 1956: 2)

Today Tanacross people see dentalium shells not only as
symbols of prestige but also as expressions of affection. One
young man said that parents express their love by sewing shells
on their children's clothing or giving them necklaces. Dentalium shells, he said, do not symbolize wealth but are "about
love."

The significance of the shells is also indicated in the
different meanings attached to the two types of dentalium
currently available. Most valuable are the old necklaces made
from Northwest Coast dentalium and handed down usually
from the father to eldest child. These are valuable not only
because they are rare but also because they reflect a history of
fundamental relationships between people. Of secondary importance are a variety of African and Japanese shells that have
been introduced within the last twenty years. Today chief's
necklaces made from Japanese dentalium are given away at
potlatches to elders in recognition of their status. They are
also occasionally sold to tourists and museums.

Like dentalium, beads are said to express affection and are
a sign of wealth. When a young man received a beaded sash
for a Christmas present, he became "bound by love" to those
who gave it to him. Beads, like dentalium, are also symbolic of
social relations that, when expressed in the form of necklaces
or sashes, literally surround or embrace the individual. When
a person wears a beaded sash or dentalium shell necklace, it is

said to be diichaagh. That is, the acknowledgment of a relationship is a great or significant act in which the wearer displays his personal status and identifies himself with his ancestor's achievements.

Historically, beads were displayed in long strings worn around the body or sewn on clothing. When a particularly prominent person died, strings of beads were broken by beating them against a building or tree in honor of the deceased. Those beads not broken were picked up by people "who had the right," that is, the paternal relatives of the deceased. William Hardisty (1872: 317–18), the Hudson Bay factor at Fort Yukon, reported the Gwich'in also destroyed beads when a person died, the relatives destroying as many of the deceased's beads as possible to indicate their grief and feelings of esteem for the dead.

Today several kinds of beaded articles are given away at potlatches. Necklaces made out of beads and "hair pipes," which are bone tubes purchased from an Indian craft supplier, are frequently distributed in lieu of dentalium shells. The woven beaded sash is another popular item that has replaced the old-style dentalium bandolier that "rich" people often wore. Other beaded objects given away include moccasins, gloves, vests, and gun cases. All of these gifts acknowledge the particular status of a guest. For instance, only leading men and women receive dentalium shell necklaces and skin garments. Articles of moose skin are also made for presentation to guests who have a special relationship to the deceased or honored person.

Guns enjoy a prestige equal to that of dentalium shells and beads, though they are a much more recent addition to Tanacross culture. Guns were introduced in the last quarter of the nineteenth century through American traders operating on the Yukon River. Tanacross oral tradition recounts that guns were introduced when a man of the Tc'a·z sib bought them from some prospectors who illustrated the power of the gun by shooting through several planks of whipsawed lumber. The Native man was so impressed that he purchased two of the guns. Through this man the guns eventually reached the Dikagiyu sib at the village of Dih thaad, who purchased the guns by piling furs to the height of the weapon, a tradition widespread in the Subarctic. The Dikagiyu bought the guns so they would be the first to own them. Apparently, prestige associated with guns is not exclusive to the Dikagiyu since the guns can also represent the Naltsiin/'Al si' dEndi' sib. Because this sib is the preferred marriage partner of the Dikagiyu in Tanacross, the gun may also symbolize an intermoiety alliance.

Guns are integral to the potlatch as gifts representing love and respect and as symbols of cultural identity. Ideally the host of a funeral potlatch would collect enough guns so there is one for the chest or torso, one for the head, one for each arm and each leg, and a seventh gun that stands for the whole body of the deceased. Additional guns collected by the host were ideally increased in increments of seven. This reflects the concern of the host to express his love and respect for the deceased by symbolically covering the body with love. Each gun metaphorically represents, or "covers," a part of the body with an object of great value "so people won't miss that person" and "have to worry about it [the body] any more."

While guns are used to cover the body with love, they are also weapons required for the hunt. It is said that "when you got no gun you can't kill anything, gun is just like food," as when a host handed the gift of a gun to a potlatch guest and he said, "Now you can kill your moose." The first guns acquired were muzzle-loading shotguns, but these are regarded today as no more than curiosities without symbolic significance. Although a variety of rifles are distributed as gifts today, the .30-.30-caliber lever action Winchester rifle is considered the "Indian gun." It is the gun associated with the autonomy of the hunting life, and it is this association that is predominant in most people's minds today.

Blankets are given away at all potlatches. They are the most numerous gifts, and it is not uncommon for three hundred or four hundred blankets to be given away at one time. Classed in two types, blankets are either considered "high-priced" or "standard." High-priced blankets are thick, white wool ones in the Hudson's Bay Company style. Prestigious and charged with emotion, real HBC blankets are rare, and only a few are given away to those people who have had a special relationship to the person being honored at the potlatch. And they are often given away in a more public display preceding the distribution of other gifts. It is also said that some of the value ascribed to HBC blankets stems from the fact that they were the first to be used in the potlatch.

It is said that "blankets is just like you put your arm around, [or] wrap somebody up with your love and warmth."[7] Giving large numbers of blankets is also thought to "cut down on a man's worry" and to make his sorrow easier. Fancy blankets, particularly the Hudson's Bay style, are always laid in and on top of the coffin. By giving an identical blanket to people especially close to the deceased, the host shares a part of the love that is buried with the dead. The emotional value of HBC blankets was expressed to me after I had given two as Christmas presents to my close friends, Elisha and Lila. Elisha said that "it was a great Indian potlatch" and that it made him feel good, almost beyond words. Lila said that when she dies she would like to be buried in hers.

Next to blankets, scarves are the most common item given away at potlatches. They may have some symbolic value similar to blankets. Purchased by the dozens, scarves are tied to rifle barrels to identify those belonging to a specific host and distributed to dancers who use them to punctuate their movements. They are also tied to grave fences as expressions of love for the dead.

Bolts of cloth, locally referred to as "calico," have been distributed at potlatches since at least the late 1920s (McKennan 1959). Occasionally cloth is hung up on the wall in display and, like scarves, is used in dancing, the dancers unraveling bolts of cloth and hanging onto it as they dance around the community hall. Afterward the lengths of cloth are torn into shorter pieces measured by stretching the cloth between both arms. The cloth is then tied in a loose knot and given away. Cloth is usually the only gender-specific gift, as it is most often only given to women, who use it for making dresses.[8]

Cash is always given away at potlatches, ordinarily in increments of $5, $10, and $20. High-ranking men and women usually receive a "package" of a rifle, a dentalium shell necklace, blankets, and cash. While there is a display around the blanket, gun, and necklace, money is handed over almost as an afterthought. Cash is also distributed to people who have assisted with the potlatch. For example, on several occasions I was given cash that compensated me for driving people to the potlatch or helping to prepare and serve food. Basically, money is distributed as a repayment for what a guest spent in attending the potlatch.

More than any other gift, however, money symbolizes a driving paradox in contemporary Native life. The most Native of institutions, the potlatch, requires that most quintessential symbol of non-Natives, money. This paradox is partially mediated by relegating money to the position of a secondary gift. Yet this mediation also serves to reinforce the power of money because, unlike the other gifts, which have been indigenized, money can never completely be co-opted as a symbol of Indianness. For this reason Native people take an apparently relaxed or disinterested view of money. I was told by one man, for instance, that for Indians money "just comes and goes." Nevertheless, money is a primary source of conflict or jealousy in the village.

The power of money is reflected in the belief that during a potlatch it can be heard moving around the hall. Money is also regarded as animate and able to generate wealth. Its power is voiced in the potlatch song that asks that "all the money in the world" be called on to "destroy the body" to alleviate the mourners' grief. Because of its power, money has to be handled carefully. A person who takes inordinate interest in wealth by continually handling it or always seeming to be involved with it in some way is suspected of being self-interested and ultimately irresponsible.

Once an object is received as a gift, it cannot be used as a gift in another potlatch by the recipient. If, however, guests wish to sell their gift, they can do so, and many gifts are sold promptly following a potlatch.[9] In a rigid sense, people are supposed to sell their gifts only if they need money. This restriction reflects a general view that potlatch gifts are supposed to be worth more than the sum of their cash value. Gifts that memorialize or acknowledge an especially close relationship or commemorate an especially important event are not sold.[10] But not all gifts are that significant. Today almost every adult attending a potlatch, regardless of who they are, receives a gift, and prominent guests may be given anywhere from two to ten blankets and two or even three guns. Consequently, some people feel no need to hold onto a gift, and they resell them either immediately after the potlatch or at some other time.

While gifts may be exchanged for cash, they do not become alienated property. It is the intention of the host to provide something of value to the guest, and if the guest feels he needs to sell it, that is his prerogative; the gift has had its use; the recipient has used it to advantage. Additionally, almost all of the gifts are sold to people who intend to make a potlatch; consequently, the object remains within the circle of distribution. Furthermore, gifts are sold well below market value. For example, a .30-.30 Winchester rifle selling at retail from $200 to $250[11] is sold for $150 at a potlatch. Hudson's Bay and Pendleton blankets retail for over $100 but are resold for $60, while common blankets are sold for $10 each regardless of their original cost. People do not want to seem greedy when selling a gift; one person's gift should not be another man's capital.

Although many people, particularly the elders, know the symbolic value of the objects discussed in this chapter, not everyone places the same value on potlatch gifts or their distribution. There are those who view the objects simply in terms of their cash value alone and, as indicated above, sell them at the first opportunity. But this attitude is not an issue in the Native community because people need cash to live. Other people associate objects and their distribution with individual power and prestige, and they involve themselves in activities, including potlatches, because they can profit either socially or economically. To this end, these people will, for example, manipulate situations either through aggressive behavior or through supernatural means to enhance their indi-

vidual position. This sort of activity is considered self-centered and irresponsible.

There is a widely shared opinion that potlatch gifts should
be purchased with a person's "own money," with money earned
through "their own hand," or with money they have a "right"
to receive. Acceptable money includes wages and government
transfer payments. The sanction against using gambling prof-
its to purchase potlatch gifts may be a result of the influence of
the Episcopal Church, which disapproved of gambling as a
corrupting influence. However, it does suggest that only by
using money obtained through one's own labor can a person
invest oneself in the gifts. Potlatch gifts, then, are multifocal
symbols that hold different meanings, depending on one's
view of the potlatch and the extent of one's participation in
the ceremony. But these differences do not indicate a complete disjuncture in the meanings associated with the gifts.
Rather, they are part of an ongoing complex reevaluation of
what is appropriate behavior. In the next chapter we will see
how these differences are acted out by the traditional leadership of the village of Tanacross.

CHAPTER 4

The Tradition Bearers
Leadership as a Reflection
of the Social Order*

Tanacross people today distinguish between two types of leaders, traditional and elected.[1] These two forms parallel changes in Native culture as well as changes in the relationship between Natives and non-Natives. The principal responsibilities of the older traditional leaders lie in organizing and leading the potlatch, while the young elected leaders, men and women in their thirties and forties, sit on the village council and village corporation board overseeing the economic development of the community. Leaders, historically, were known as "rich men,"[2] responsible for organizing the acquisition, accumulation, and redistribution of resources by which they validated and maintained their prestige and gained approval to lead (McKennan 1959; Guedon 1974; Strong 1972). Today these economic tasks are directed by young elected leaders charged, by law, with acquiring and managing the community's resources, including those allocated by state and local government. This has left the traditional leaders the place of "tradition bearers," proponents and exemplars of the Indian way.

*This title is derived from Ellanna and Balluta (1992: 268).

Differences in types of contemporary leadership reflect the contradictions and conflicts of modern Native identity. There are the young, educated, elected leaders whose major focus is competence within the non-Native world. None is sufficiently experienced in traditional life to enable them to play a leading role in the potlatch. Their primary sphere of influence is the village council and Tanacross village corporation.

The village council has its roots in Episcopal missionary and U.S. government policies. In an effort to formalize leadership, the Church, in 1912, organized the election of a chief and a council of elders who, in conjunction with the missionary, kept order in the village. After the Indian Reorganization Act was extended to Alaska in 1936 (Case 1984: 99), the council became the legal governing body of the village. Today it consists of six elected members: president, secretary, treasurer, and three councillors.[3] Their primary duties are administering village improvement grants, made available by federal and state agencies, and representing village interests at the state and regional levels. Councillors also have the authority to pass laws regulating people's behavior in the village, especially regarding the use of alcohol.

Distinct from the village council, the Tanacross Native Corporation was established under the Alaska Native Land Claims Act of 1971. Unlike the IRA council, which is the legally recognized government of the village, Tanacross Incorporated is a profit-making business with an elected board of directors and president. Assets include land and cash received through the Alaska Native Claims Settlement Act. Because the village population is small, membership on both the council and the corporation board overlaps to a degree. Currently membership of both bodies is composed of men and women whose average age is about forty-two. Several members have received university training, and all have a wide range of work experience outside the village.

In contrast, the older, more traditionally experienced elders and leaders are competent in the Indian way, which, for them, is a lived reality. Though isolated from the complexities of modern bureaucratic life, principally because of their lack of formal education, traditional leaders have played, and continue to play, important roles in determining the future direction of the village. Currently one traditional leader acts as an adviser to the village council and keeps abreast of all local activity. As adviser he does not have access to resources available to the council or board of directors but is able to exert some influence on how those resources are allocated once they become available in the village.

Traditional leadership derives its authority not merely from a communal respect or nostalgia for the past but also from what it has accomplished. Much of the present land claims settlement, for example, is the legacy of the older generation who feels it was accomplished by maintaining and asserting the Indian way. Andrew Isaac, traditional chief of the Tanana Chiefs Conference Incorporated, the nonprofit regional corporation formed under ANCSA, symbolizes this older generation. Paraphrasing one man,

> Andrew is important because he has hung on to his "Indian life." When Andrew dies the people at Tanana Chiefs will have to settle for the law whereas Andrew is now able to block the Whites by keeping an Indian focus on the issues. (From field notes collected in Tanacross, 1987)[4]

Elders such as the speaker above fear that the younger leaders will lose the land and, what is even more alarming, will have to become like non-Natives. They think that the young, despite their education and experience in the non-Native world, are unable to compete in it. Not surprisingly, they regard the "Indian life," or the Indian way, as crucial. It is the message that the elders and traditional leaders feel competent to teach, and it is the basis for the structure that ensures them of some control and continued relevance.

Even though there have been substantial changes in the nature of traditional leadership, there is continuity in the ways a modern tradition bearer can validate his leadership. Through his individual example, he leads the village in moments of crisis, especially at funerals and potlatches. He is expected to be generous and smart and to possess verbal eloquence or some skill indicating knowledge and understanding of tradition. The tradition bearer validates his authority and enhances his prestige through responsible acts that show his concern for the people. He has other duties that are not so clearly defined, and performance varies with the individual. In this respect traditional leadership is a developing institution in which both the people and the leader forge a synthesis on how to fulfill this role.

Among the tradition bearers of Tanacross are two men, Elisha and Jack, both of the 'Al si' dEndi' sib, who are the ranking men of two groups that trace their paternal descent from two important leading men, Tsiint-le' and Ket-laata'. Because of their backgrounds, both Elisha and Jack play historical roles that are affected both by people's expectations and by each man's personal synthesis of the Indian way.

Although each man is a tradition bearer in his own way, the focus and activity of their leadership is very different. As the older of the two, Elisha has already attained leader status; he is a well-respected elder who has given many potlatches and "can talk well for his people." His leadership rests in his synthesis of Christian spirituality and the ideals of the Indian way. By contrast, the thrust of Jack's leadership reflects his concern for the material welfare of his community. To this end, he is energetically involved in a wide variety of village activities ranging from the Christmas party to the organization of the annual village-sponsored dogsled race, the annual "survival camp," and potlatches. For Jack, the potlatch appears to be an important means to enhance the community's physical and material well-being. The histories of these two men exemplify much of the history of leadership in Tanacross, which is also a history of their families. Without the appropriate background evident from their descent group, neither Elisha nor Jack could legitimize or validate his leadership. The differences in leadership arise out of the history of the people and their changing relations with non-Natives.

CHANGING LEADERSHIP: 1867–1912

Historically, Upper Tanana society was based on a system of rank. At the top were rich men who, through marriages with three or more women,[5] had influence over a whole village or a number of smaller villages.[6] The importance of these rich men is reflected in the fact that they are identified precisely in the genealogical record (Guedon 1974: 141) as the progenitors or "grandfathers" of the people. In this respect rich men were considered bigger than life. They were not simply manifestations of social norms; in their achievements, they were considered superlative, providing examples of behavior unattainable by the majority (Ellanna and Balluta (1992: 268). Next in rank were less influential sub-chiefs who had only one or two wives and represented their people's interests on the local level only. Also included as men of rank were shamans, or "sleep doctors" (Guedon 1974: 141; Strong 1972: chap. 3:25–27).

A rich man's position and authority were based both on ascribed status and on achievement.[7] One of the leader's greatest assets was his sib affiliation (see McClellan 1975: 490 for the Tutchone). Belonging to a high-ranking sib gave the leader access to knowledge acquired through physical and mental training received from older male relatives, particularly his mother's brothers. Not only did a leader inherit knowledge but he also inherited the symbols of leadership, such as dentalium shell necklaces, which made it easier to legitimize his authority. Moreover, if a leader was a ranking individual of a numerically well-represented and high-ranking sib,[8] his ability to achieve and maintain a position of power was greatly enhanced. But a leader also had to show remarkable ability at managing resources to sustain his leadership over his sibmates. If he was particularly able, he could attract a number of marriage partners and in this way extend influence over his wives' siblings as well.[9]

The major responsibilities of the old-fashioned rich men involved organizing and managing economic activities, particularly the communal caribou hunts and trading expeditions, and redistributing the products acquired from these activities (Strong 1972: chap. 5:29). Avenues for redistributing food and goods were community feasts and the potlatch. The latter was particularly important in validating and enhancing a leader's prestige. Through a potlatch, a leader could demonstrate his ability to accumulate goods as well as his generosity. Leader's were also responsible for finding wives for their followers, for giving them aid and protection (ibid., chap. 3:25–27), for settling disputes, and for making speeches concerning their welfare. In return, a leader could call on his relatives to donate goods for a mortuary ceremony, to offer support in war, or to back him up in the event of a disagreement. Essentially, the leader and his followers shared a reciprocal relationship in which the former was expected to care for both the spiritual and the material needs of his people, who in turn responded with their labor and support in critical periods such as war. [10]

In Tanacross history, two such leaders were Tsiint-le' and Ket-laata'. Of the two, Tsiint-le' appears to have been the most important, although Ket-laata' is the only one mentioned in the historical record. Tsiint-le' was called "boss" and *Tsey sh ann*, meaning "old grandpa," and it was he who directed the people in building the caribou fences and the great communal hunts. Tsiint-le' lived at Dih thaad but was from a place called Flint Rock, about four miles south of Ketchumstuk. [11] Tsiint-le' is considered a great leader, although he is remembered as having a bad temper. No one knows when Tsiint-le' or Ket-laata' died.

In 1900, the Tanacross people were apparently divided into two local exogamous bands centered on two semipermanent villages, Mansfield and Ketchumstuk. The two bands had overlapping subsistence areas and close affinal ties. The Mansfield band was led by Sam Thomas (b. ca. 1851–d. 1939), a member of the Dikagiyu sib and the ranking elder brother of a core group of siblings who were maternal nieces and nephews of Tsiint-le' and Ket-laata'. Both Thomas and his brother married upper Ahtna women who, along with several of their siblings, came to live at Mansfield. [12] At the same time, all or part of the Ketchumstuk band appears to have been led by another rich man named Isaac (b. ca. 1849–d. 1912) who is said to have been a headman of the Naltsiin sib. Born near the mouth of the

Goodpaster River, downriver from Tanacross, Isaac, as a young man, moved with his family to Ts'eyh Ketlaagh', or "Boat Bottom," which is at the head of Healy River. From there the family moved to Joseph Village, called Jiiz Ndiig, or "Camp Robber Creek" (Yarber and Madison 1988: 3), to be closer to traders located on the Yukon and Fortymile rivers. Isaac eventually married a woman from Ketchumstuk, and his nephews married high-ranking women from Mansfield, including one of Sam Thomas's sisters. Thus by about 1900, Sam Thomas and his siblings had made marriage alliances with Upper Ahtna and Goodpaster people. From these marriages are derived the major families of modern Tanacross.

As rich men, both Sam Thomas and Isaac were responsible for managing resources, particularly the long caribou snare fences that crisscrossed the region. Isaac was called the boss for a portion of a snare fence and large caribou surround near Ketchumstuk (Paul 1974: 16), while Sam Thomas had several snare fences that he may have inherited from his uncle, Tsiintle'.[13] Both men were able to mobilize and organize the labor of their kinsmen, which was the key to maintaining a leader's position (Strong 1972: chap. 3:25–27).

Isaac's prominence was enhanced through his involvement with the Episcopal Church (Stuck 1913). According to Church records, he was responsible for the establishment of the mission at Tanacross, which was opened in 1912, the year Isaac died (McIntosh 1941: 3). As a result, the Church bestowed on him the title of chief, much as trading captains or trading chiefs were named by the Hudson's Bay Company. Isaac's importance to the missionary cause is reflected in the references to Chief Isaac in the Episcopal Church literature of the time. Sam Thomas, by contrast, appears in one brief note with an accompanying photograph.

On Chief Isaac's death in 1912, a large potlatch, attended by guests from Mentasta, Tetlin, Ketchumstuk, and Moosehide, a Han Athapaskan village located near present-day Dawson City, was held in his honor (Stuck 1913: 85). After Isaac's death, his son Walter, a member of the Dikagiyu sib, took over as chief. According to a history of the mission written by the Reverend E. A. McIntosh (1941: 6), Walter was selected chief in an election arranged by the missionaries. Tanacross people, however, point out that Walter in fact inherited the position. In staging the election, the intentions of the missionaries were fairly clear. They sought to break the influence of the traditional leaders, whose authority depended on their ascribed status and personal achievement, and assert the moral and secular authority of the Church by designating a leader through democratic means.[14]

In addition to his traditional duties, Walter became the first leader of the village council, which consisted of a number of leading men who met with various outside entities, including the Church. Through the council, the Church attempted to regulate certain aspects of the Native people's lives, including the potlatch and later the consumption of alcohol. Chief Walter and the council were also involved with John Hajdukovich's abortive attempt to establish a reserve around Tanacross in the 1930s, and they negotiated with the U.S. military when it decided to upgrade the Tanacross airport at the beginning of World War II. In the mid-1960s, Chief Walter also led the fight to stop the state of Alaska from selling land that was claimed by Tanacross.

After Chief Walter died in 1965, his elder brother's son, Andrew Isaac, a member of the Naltsiin sib, became chief. Subsequently, Andrew became heavily involved in land claims negotiations and eventually became traditional chief of Doyon Ltd., the regional corporation established by the Alaska Native Claims Settlement Act. Oscar Isaac, Andrew's first cousin, took over Andrew's position as chief and is now a highly esteemed and widely recognized tradition bearer and leader in Tanacross and in the Upper Tanana Region.

The recognition of Isaac as chief by the Church and the subsequent "election" of his son, Walter, created a long-term tension in the community. At an earlier time competition must have existed between two such obviously dynamic men as Isaac and Sam Thomas, both of whom were listed as chief on the 1910 census of Mansfield village. Today disagreement exists between the descendants of Isaac and Sam Thomas as to who was and was not a chief. Although couched in historical terms, this dispute concerns competition over prestige and prominence in the village today. On some occasions the village becomes aligned along the descent lines emanating from these old chiefs, now represented by Jack and Elisha. These divisions, not always apparent, are real because they do affect people's actions. This dispute is important in terms of traditional leadership because there is no clear status distinction between the present tradition bearers. Currently, Jack and Elisha are both prominent men who have two distinct leadership patterns.

CONTEMPORARY LEADERSHIP

A man in his fifties, Jack's hair is shot with gray. He is of middle height, heavyset, and with a clean-shaven face. He is married and has five children and ten grandchildren. Jack attends church infrequently and at one time played poker and bingo regularly. He has stopped drinking, as many men of his generation have, by simply making up his mind not to drink.

He hunts moose during the season, but he does not trap or fish. He is fluent in the Tanacross language and in English. During the late 1960s and 1970s, Jack worked for a U.S. government agency where he learned skills as a leader and acquired experience dealing with non-Natives at various levels. From these experiences Jack developed a particular rapport with non-Natives. He often invites non-Native people from Tok to attend village feasts, both as a show of generosity and to maintain friendly contacts with the non-Native community.

Jack has a particular interest in the general development of the village, and on that score he participates in a variety of activities. As an elder, he acts as an adviser to the Tanacross village council. He is instrumental in organizing various village activities such as the annual dogsled race, the two riverboat races sponsored by the village, and the annual Christmas and Fourth of July parties. According to Jack, these activities are important both for keeping up community spirit and for enhancing the prestige of the village, since people from other villages are invited. During the summer he takes a prominent part in the organization of the annual survival camp held for the Tanacross children at the old village of Mansfield.

Jack's involvement in these affairs is based on his willingness and talent to organize and mobilize a wide network of people including family, relatives, and friends. To organize an event, he first involves his immediate family, especially his children, then nephews and friends, whom he feels comfortable asking for help. His major support, however, derives from his eldest daughter, a member of the Dikagiyu sib, who displays the organizational talents of her father. She often assumes responsibility for organizing community events when no one else will, and she is the only young person who speaks publicly at potlatches and other gatherings. Beyond his children, Jack also relies on a wide network of sib relations and maternal relatives from which he derives legitimacy and strength as a tradition bearer.

This network is apparent in Jack's participation in funerals and potlatches. In a funeral and potlatch for his paternal aunt, for instance, Jack, active as the principal organizer, collected donations, purchased food, and organized the construction of the coffin, grave fence, and moose hunt. To facilitate transportation of the food purchased in Tok, he borrowed a truck from a local non-Native entrepreneur married to a woman from the village. At the same time he borrowed the truck, Jack enlisted the man's help in cooking breakfasts for the potlatch. For constructing the grave fence, he enlisted the help of his son-in-law and a local non-Native man who lives in the village and is a skillful carpenter. Additionally, Jack also saw to numerous details including purchasing shovels and axes used for digging the grave and the paint and nails for constructing the grave fence, coffin, and overbox. He also represented the village and family in negotiations with the local magistrate over the burial of the body. Though he played no public role in the church funeral service, he had mobilized every resource and connection he could to make the funeral and subsequent potlatch a success.

In the early stages of preparing for the funeral, Jack automatically took the lead by building a consensus around his leadership. He consulted the other 'Al si' dEndi' headman, Elisha, to determine who should participate and what should be done. During this discussion, it was plain that Jack was in charge and that Elisha, after stating his position, would follow his lead. He consulted other leading people about the time of the funeral, including Elisha's wife, Lila, who is Jack's sister-in-law and an important Dikagiyu woman.

Jack was also very much involved in the potlatch after the funeral. During potlatches, various headmen take different roles depending on their abilities or predilections. Jack's forte is singing, drumming, and dancing, and he often shares the lead, along with several other men and women, in these activities. With other men and women, he sits in one corner of the community hall warming up his voice and practicing until the whole group bursts forth with song as members of the audience get up to join in. Once out on the floor, Jack's enthusiasm and energy are apparent as he encourages people to dance and sing.

At one potlatch, staged by two widows who had no one to lead for them, Jack filled the role of dance leader. When the potlatch hostesses and their families came out on the floor to open the dancing, Jack urged them on with his drumming. He then handed the drum to the grandson of one of the women and joined the crowd on the dance floor as he continued to urge everyone on. Whenever the singing died away, Jack, in a voice heard above everyone else's, started a new song to keep the singing from flagging. If people stopped dancing, Jack gently pushed and shoved them to get them moving again. In this way, he inspired people to "break out the good time."

Jack often assists the hosts in distributing their gifts by pointing out people who should be acknowledged. At one potlatch, after the more important gifts had been distributed by the hosts, Jack helped the hosts to distribute their gifts, handing out blankets in stacks of five to all of the guests. At another potlatch, he helped the hosts draw up a list of recipients, watched them give the major gifts away, and then helped them to distribute the rest. The one thing Jack does not do during a potlatch is speak publicly. This silence may be indicative of Jack's current capacity as a leader. He is confi-

dent in his ability to organize behind the scenes and to sing
and dance, but he is still lacks the knowledge, and possibly the
confidence, required for giving a speech.

Jack's practicality, conspicuous energy, and willingness to
adapt tradition to the current world is in contrast to Elisha's
quieter, spiritually oriented leadership. At age seventy-five,
Elisha is perhaps ten or twelve years older than Jack, and
though sedentary, he retains remarkable vigor. For a number
of years, he was custodian of the Tanacross elementary school,
and he did a short stint on the Alaska pipeline project. But his
main occupation until his retirement was trapping. Also an
active and avid moose hunter, he is out on the land during
moose season.

Elisha's role as leader and elder is founded in part on his
participation in community affairs. At one time he was active
on the village council, and he has given a number of potlatches for relatives, including three of his adult children who
died in accidents. Through this Elisha has forged a leadership
that centers less on activity than spiritual guidance. Not that
Elisha is uninvolved in village affairs or uninterested or
unconcerned with the prestige that derives from leadership.
Rather, Elisha's approach is low-key, and he attempts to lead
by example.

This means that he regularly attends Church as well as a
Bible study class conducted in the Tanacross language by a
local Wycliffe Bible translator. He does not gamble or drink,
though he once did both. Elisha attends potlatches and
dances and sings there, but he is never conspicuous in these
activities. He does, however, make speeches, which are in-
formed by both his understanding of Christianity and his
knowledge of traditional ways. In a speech he may, depending
on whom he is talking to, combine Christian tolerance and

expressions of love with very subtle references to his prestige and position as a leader. If, for example, he is talking to nonsib members, as he did at a potlatch in Chistochina, he is very modest because he realizes that it is important to maintain good relations, particularly with nonrelatives. But if he speaks to his relations, or sibmates, as he did one time at a funeral for a murdered man, he is very blunt and forceful. As one woman said, Elisha will speak his mind and not be afraid to "just tell you off." Such honesty and sensitivity to people and situations gives him enormous prestige and validity as a leader.

In attempting to understand the present situation of Native people, Elisha has created categories of how to live. Though distinct, the Indian way, the non-Native way, and the Christian way are not mutually exclusive.[15] According to Elisha, and I paraphrase here, what is good about non-Native people is that they take care of themselves. They are concerned with making a good living and being responsible for themselves instead of fighting, drinking, and getting into trouble with the law. The problem is that non-Natives are too self-centered and concerned only with money. Native people, by contrast, especially the young, do not act responsibly, either toward themselves or others. If a person takes care of himself, makes a good living, behaves, and does not go to jail, he "might get back on the Indian way"; that is, he might start to straighten himself out. To be an Indian, however, a man must also act responsibly toward his relatives and meet his obligations as a member of the community. If an individual can do this, he can then give himself to God and "turn to be a Christian." In essence, Elisha believes that Native people should take care of themselves and their relatives, be responsible to the community, and believe in God.

The problem, as Elisha sees it, is a lack of belief. He sees most people in the Native community as believing in nothing, not in being Native, Christian, or non-Native. This skepticism has made him very critical of his own people, and this criticism has earned him reproach. Elisha believes that few Native people really understand the potlatch, nor are they really interested in living like "real" Natives. People have trivialized the potlatch to the point that it has no more meaning than a community dinner in Tok. In Elisha's eyes, the potlatch is "alive," so powerful that it can actually kill someone if he does not pay attention to the supernatural restrictions that accompany the performance of a potlatch. As he puts it,

> That's the way the potlatch go, potlatch is awfully great, really important to the Native life. Really be careful for all the young girls got to watch themself, like young girls have month sick, not supposed to be coming in there, otherwise, if they do, don't watch themselves they going to die quick, some way they going to get into trouble and die. For that part there's lots of injih [meaning the potential for bad luck] in potlatch. Potlatch have more *injih* than anything, any kind of injih in the world. They got take care, certain way for long life. If we don't take care right, the people going to die outa that place. (Interview recorded in Tanacross, September 1987)

What Elisha sees as the absence of belief, either in the strictures of the Indian way or in Christianity, is one reason he thinks Native people are having such a difficult time now. Lack of belief pulls them into alcoholism and other destructive behavior. Despite these criticisms of his people, Elisha has not withdrawn from participation in the potlatch or village life. He insists that the potlatch is important, and he often says that he goes to potlatches to learn from the speeches made by men older than he.

PERCEPTIONS OF MODERN LEADERSHIP

As noted above, old-fashioned rich men were considered bigger than life in that they were considered exemplars of behavior unattainable by the average person (Ellanna and Balluta 1992: 268). Modern traditional leaders too are supposed to exhibit behavior that is exemplary. For this reason there is no consensus concerning the traditional leadership of the village. Some people say there is no chief, while others say that Elisha is the old chief and Jack aspires to be chief. While much of this disagreement has historical roots, it is also based on the perceptions people have about the kind of men Elisha and Jack are. As one woman put it, Jack appears too ambitious and Elisha is now just getting to the age where he could be chief. The most important attribute for a chief, she thinks, is the ability "to talk well." Elisha would be a good chief because he can speak his mind. The woman's reservations about Jack stem from his overly aggressive involvement in community affairs, something a good chief does not do. Despite these misgivings, many people feel that Jack, because of his age and experience and Elisha's health, will be the next traditional leader. As another woman said during a potlatch, she was afraid the people would be lost after the old people died and felt Jack was the only one who could "hold the people up" or continue with the old ways.

Ideally, a leader is supposed to "love" the people, be "friendly" and kindly," be able to settle disputes by talking to people, and "talk well" for the people in general. He should also be competent, that is, know how to take care of himself and those he leads. Sib affiliation, or "formal background," knowledge, and discipline are also mentioned as prerequisites for leadership. A young man wrote the following description of what is expected of a modern traditional leader.

The people of the village don't all at once race toward leadership[,] each and everyone had to have reputation of formal background and discipline[.] Village leaders are [those men] who hold the interest of their people and have [the] capability to handle all small to biggest problem, or problems, within village or elsewhere[.] [L]oving for their own [people] has been one of the requirements [as well]. (From a written statement collected in Tanacross, 1987)

A man from Tetlin described the importance of having a traditional chief this way:

If no chief, we don't get anybody to boss, to teach us. They have to have a good man to watch the children, tell us what to do, tell us how to make party [i.e., a potlatch]. He let us know to everybody where to go hunt, when they go hunting; he watches and checks them when they come back. . . . You got to have one chief. (Guedon 1974: 145)

No one in Tanacross entirely fills this bill. The traditional roles and expertise of the elders and leaders have been eroded by external political and economic forces. Current challenges of economic development, investment, and political leadership on a wider stage are beyond the abilities of the older tradition bearers. They have neither the knowledge nor the experience. One young woman told me that today Tanacross needs a strong leader, one who will stand up for the rights of the people. She believed that in the past people respected the old chief, but his power was undermined by the Bureau of Indian Affairs, which made all the decisions. Now there is no strong leader who can make sound investment decisions concerning the land and money Tanacross has or who can make decisions regarding Native rights.

These ambivalent comments on the state of the current leadership reflect the paradox of contemporary Native life. On one hand, people want someone who is aggressive and able to look after their increasingly complex economic interests. On the other hand, they also want someone capable of "holding them up," of representing and maintaining tradition. Aggressive, pragmatic behavior is acceptable if it appears not to be entirely motivated by self-interest. There is a consensus that economic development is essential and that well-organized community activities, including potlatches, bring prestige to the village. There is also a strong sense that the actions of the elders are necessary for providing a coherent vision of the Athapaskan world and ensuring continuity of the group. But the spiritual and emotional expressions of the potlatch should not be reduced to economics or exploited in the quest for personal prestige.

Tradition becomes important in this context because it is perceived to be above economic and social competition. It also serves to maintain a coherent backdrop by which people can gauge their own and other people's behavior. But while tradition serves as an objective for ideal behavior, it is felt to be too confining. For example, restrictions on young women participating in the potlatch are no longer acceptable to many of the young women influenced by feminism. Further, these restrictions are not practical now since it is the young women who are taking increasing responsibility in village activities, including the potlatch. Many people, especially the young, believe that tradition is outmoded because it is detached from the practical aspects of modern life.

Traditional leadership nevertheless continues to be a vital aspect of contemporary village life. How it leads, what cultural message it creates and communicates, is open to continual negotiation. We have seen how two leaders, using tradition and individual experience in the non-Native world, have developed personal syntheses of the Indian way. Each in his own way has indicated what he feels to be the road of the future for the Tanacross people. In the next chapter we see what constitutes the Indian way.

CHAPTER 5

Images of
Native and Non-Native
Components of Contemporary Identity

This chapter concerns the images Tanacross people have of themselves and of non-Natives. Derived from the major conceptual opposition of Indian versus non-Native, these images are further categorized as oppositions of "real" versus "modern Native" and "old whites" versus "new whites." It is in these broad terms, Indian and non-Native and present versus past, that the potlatch becomes important as a point of mediation. The potlatch represents the past and defines real Native life, which is nonwhite. By participating in the potlatch, Native people try to maintain and reproduce what they consider to be the real image of their traditional culture: kinship, reciprocity, generosity, "love and respect," and competence.[1] In these themes, which embody the Indian way, people maintain not only the image of their Indianness but also their distinctiveness from non-Natives. But this simple explanation belies the ambiguous and contradictory nature of the situation.

Some contemporary Native people consider themselves less as real Natives and more like non-Natives. This paradox was graphically described to me two days after I arrived in

Tanacross to do fieldwork in December 1987. Jack, an older leader, held up his hands about two feet apart. One hand stood for the old way of life; the other stood for the non-Native way. His people, he said, were situated somewhere in between: though he is closer to the Indian way, his children are closer to the non-Native way. Natives are lost because they do not live like real Indians, and they are not strong enough or know how to lead that kind of life again. Still they can never be white people.

"Instead of living in tents like 'real' Indians," Jack said, "we live in houses; instead of moving from place to place, we live in one place and have summer cabins; instead of a 'few groceries,' we have plenty of store food; and instead of 'walking fifty miles a day on snowshoes,' we sit at home." Furthermore, "people have social security benefits and retirement plans." Paradoxically, Jack maintains that an Indian could never be white, nor a white, Indian.

Though modern Indians are not "real," there are aspects of real Native culture that Jack believes must be continued. The "tribes" or sibs are important because people have to know whom to marry. The potlatch is important as well, though Jack did not say why. Kin ties are important, and he emphasized this by telling me that he is related to almost all of the people in Tanacross as well as people from the neighboring villages of Tetlin and the Copper River.[2]

Jack's view, I think, reflects the general perception of most Tanacross people. Another man, for instance, told me that today there are no "genuine" Indians. Instead people are one-half or three-fourths Native depending, not on blood, but on how far away they are from the "old time." In the future he thought that Native life would become progressively more non-Native and that all the information stored in libraries would not help the people live the Indian life. This pessimism reflects not just an apparent loss of culture or exploitation by non-Natives, but an acute sense that people have lost control of their own lives. Still, Native American people are attempting to maintain some coherence in the face of the ambiguities and contradictions that beset their present lives. The past, embodied in the Indian way, acts as an anchor that, even if people feel they themselves changing, is a point from which to gauge that change and as a way of life to emulate and maintain.

The Indian way is a response to the feeling of being lost; it is based on an ideal model of social relations emphasizing kinship, reciprocity, generosity, love, and respect. By asserting the importance of these aspects of Native life, Jack and many others maintain a notion of society in which the individual person takes on meaning only in the context of a web of relationships. Social relations are based on a definite hierarchy according to degree of relation and age. Maturity comes with increasing awareness of natural and supernatural relationships and the prescriptions and proscriptions for proper behavior. A person in pursuit of his or her individual gratification, without regard for others, loses sight of his or her role and as a result, loses, either figuratively or literally, his or her humanity.

Both as tradition and a model for action, the Indian way constitutes a positive image. But it is also a reminder of how people really are. Though they strive to maintain the Indian way, they believe they are becoming more like non-Natives. This irony is enhanced by the internal contradictions within Native society produced by economic competition and a reinterpretation of traditional values. Although there may be a consensus on certain aspects of Native identity, it is con-

stantly being reinterpreted as individuals relate to and inter-
act with the broader economic, political, and cultural changes
occurring in North American culture.[3] According to some
villagers, these contradictions have several sources. One is
"jealousy" over economic success. Jealousy over money causes
people to become stingy and uncaring, that is, like non-
Natives. People become envious over someone else's ability to
purchase a new car. Another source of contradiction is differences in experience and age. Old people are usually conserva-
tive and advocate being competent first in the Indian way and
then in the non-Native world. For them, all aspects of the
Indian way are relevant. Most middle-aged people tend to be
less rigid about the Indian way. For them, competence in the
non-Native world takes precedence because it is the world
they work in. Though not completely irrelevant, the Indian
way does not hold their full attention. It is, in many respects,
an ideal to be respected rather than a way of life. At the
extreme end of the spectrum are those who see the Indian way
as completely irrelevant. These are principally young people
whose major concern is to get out of the village, which some
compare to a corral. One man went so far as to declare that
soon there will be no Indians because Native culture is only
concerned with the past and all of the young people are going
to run away.[4]

Young people are leaving, and they have one major desti-
nation: the world of the non-Native.[5] They soon learn that
the relationship between Natives and non-Natives is fraught
with misunderstandings and contradictions. As one woman
said, non-Natives demand that Natives live like them, but
when Natives try, non-Natives give them a hard time. Native
people know they have been and continue to be subjugated by
non-Natives even though the ideology of the United States

insists that everyone is equal. Though people, mostly the young, move away from the village, they retain a profound and ineradicable attachment to it. Very few Native people move away from the village for long periods of time, and even fewer cut off their relationships completely.

"OLD WHITE" AND "NEW WHITE": CHANGING RELATIONS

Native people have drawn from their historical experience two contrasting images of non-Native people, characterized as "old whites" and "new whites." Old whites are those who lived in the Upper Tanana Region prior to World War II; new whites are more recent arrivals. Relations with old whites were based on a sense of equality and reciprocal obligation that Natives feel is lacking in their relationship with new whites. Native perceptions of these old relations is illustrated in a story about the trader John Hajdukovich, who once extended considerable credit to Chief John for the purchase of potlatch goods. All winter, according to the story, Hajdukovich worried about how the chief was going to pay what he owed, how he was going to catch enough fur. When summer came, Hajdukovich was greeted by Chief John, who told him to come to his cache. There he pulled out sacks of fur, so many that Hajdukovich owed the chief money. [6]

This story illustrates a number of themes in historic Native–non-Native relations. The relationship between Chief John and Hajdukovich is viewed in terms of generalized reciprocity in which the equality of each participant is acknowledged (on generalized reciprocity, see Sahlins 1972; cf. Bently 1987: 42). Chief John not only repays Hajdukovich, he actually gives more than he owes, so, in Native parlance, he "beats" the trader, who becomes indebted. But non-Natives are also seen as greedy. Hajdukovich "worries" about his money, a typical attribute of non-Natives, while Natives are viewed as competent and moral; they always fulfill their obligations by repaying their debts. Additionally, the relationship is based on a face-to-face interaction; these men knew each other. It is this intimacy, which also involves respect and equality, that many Native people feel is lacking in contemporary Native–non-Native relations. [7]

Reciprocal relations between old whites and Natives extended to other spheres as well. Missionaries, miners, and traders, for instance, are remembered for helping Natives learn English and about the outside world. They also gave Natives "groceries" when they were lacking resources, as well as pieces of dried meat that non-Natives did not want. [8] In return, Natives gave non-Natives moccasins and mittens and taught them how to survive during the winter. But the most important attribute of "old-time whites" was their apparent respect for Native people. This respect was evident, at least in Native eyes, because old-time non-Natives lived like Natives, ate Native food, spent time with Natives, and lived off the land like "real" Natives. They "knew how hard life was for Natives and so respected Native people and felt kindly toward them."[9]

Native perceptions of non-Natives changed after the end of World War II. With the development of the Alaska Highway, Native people were pushed into a backwater and left in the same conditions as when they had first moved from their camps on the land. Non-Natives who migrated into the area took military and civilian jobs in the new town of Tok Junction. Face-to-face relationships became limited to a particularly narrow social sphere that non-Natives dominated, such as bars, stores, and schools. Young people attending high school in Tok came face-to-face with the harsh racism found previously only in towns such as Fairbanks, Nome, and Anchorage. Only the missionaries[10] and a few non-Native social workers continued to meet Native people in the village. As a consequence, the social distance between Natives and new whites increased to the extent that they no longer know each other, and as a result, both Natives and non-Natives have constructed largely negative images of one another (Braroe 1975).

According to Elisha, "White people changed [and] they were not as kind as old whites, not as friendly [or] cared for Native people." Elisha qualified this statement when he said that new whites are good to Natives, "[p]robably a lot more good to Native, [but] it doesn't show because whites don't stay around."[11] Elisha acknowledges that new whites assist Natives in many ways. What has changed, in his view, is the social distance between them. Before the war, Natives and non-Natives inhabited an overlapping universe of shared experiences based on life close to the land and characterized by face-to-face interactions. After the war, this universe was fragmented and Native people became socially, economically, and politically marginalized.

Whether or not all people in Tanacross agree with Elisha's perceptions, and I think many would, today most Native people characterize contemporary non-Natives as individualistic and selfish. In Native terms, in addition to being worried only about money and jealous of one another's success (something village people also accuse each other of), non-Natives are thought to be jealous of Natives for getting land and money under the Alaska Native Claims Settlement Act and receiving social benefits from the federal government.

Non-Natives are also viewed as being concerned with "making a good living" and of taking "care of [their] money"

and getting "into business and get rich." They are interested primarily in taking care of themselves as individuals
and not as members of a circle of consanguineous, affinal,
and sib relationships.[12] It is through the potlatch that
Native people express their attachment to one another.
Non-Natives, according to Elisha, "don't handle potlatch,"
meaning that non-Natives, when they make money, do not
use it to maintain reciprocal obligations or to honor their
relatives. He added that if an "Indian made a lot of money
and didn't use it for potlatch then some Indians might make
fun of him."

This negative image of the non-Native contrasts with the
attitude Native people have toward the former's general economic success, which they attribute to an apparently natural
business ability and a competitive, ambitious nature. These
characteristics are both admired and criticized. On a broad
level, where, for instance, Native regional and village corporations created by ANCSA have to compete to stay solvent,
competitiveness and business acumen are admired and in fact
demanded. On the village level, however, these same characteristics are condemned, and in regard to the potlatch particularly, competition is considered anathema because the potlatch is about "love" rather than "jealousy" or competition.

Finally, Native people believe new non-Natives have no
respect for them. This disrespect, evident in racist lore, of
which Native people are well aware, portrays them as generally dirty, drunk, and having lost their culture. In response,
Native people have attempted to maintain a positive image by
publicly reproducing the real Indian values of kinship, generosity, reciprocity, love, respect, and competence, which are
the Indian way. Within this framework the Indian way becomes both a bridge between the past and the present and an

ideology stressing the superiority of Native life, the old over the young, and experience in the Indian way over the education of the non-Native.

THE INDIAN WAY

Kinship

A major theme in Native "discourse" on the Indian way, kinship is integral to placing people within a hierarchical structure based on age and degree of relatedness.[13] In contrast to non-Natives, Native people think of themselves as relying on their relatives for assistance rather than on only themselves and on "money." Kinship, then, is a key symbol in the image of real Indian culture and community.

Knowing and maintaining the intricate genealogical ties that unite village and region are important because people have to know whom to marry and to whom potlatch gifts are to be distributed. In Tanacross, the ideal and most politically advantageous marriages are considered, by the elders, to be between cross-cousins of the Dikagiyu and Naltsiin/'Al si' dEndi' sibs. Explaining the marriage system, Elisha said that by raising his wife's children, who are Dikagiyu as she is, "he worked for nothing" because when the children grew up they would "go back to their head people." Elisha's work would "come back" through his son's children, who are "worth more" to him because they would belong to his sib.

Each sib reproduces and reinforces the other by creating two powerful localized lineages allied by many marriages (Heinrich 1957; Guedon 1974: 86).[14] In this configuration, both parental links become significant, and the most prominent people in Native society are those who can boast of being the product of a long line of correct marriages. Furthermore, a superior lineage gives prominence even to the poorest of people. One Tanacross man points out,

> Because I come from those people, because I come from those people like Sam Thomas [a Dikagiyu headman] and his daddy and all those people at Mansfield, because they are my grandfather, *if today Indian feel like those days,* even if I am poor, they know I am poor man, people will respect me, just on account of those people before me. That's the Indian feeling of those people, even if I got nothing. . . . I still come from those people and people just respect me for that. (Interview recorded November 1987; emphasis added)

As the narrator says, however, people do not "feel like those days," that is, as they did in the past. For many people, especially the young, the intricacies of correct behavior dictated by the kinship system seem increasingly irrelevant. Although many people may believe that knowing and maintaining the "old ways" is irrelevant on one level, on another level, the kinship system is a very significant symbol of community. Community based on kinship derives, in part, from people's image of the past. In the following quotation, a senior woman from Dot Lake, Alaska, explains the importance of relatives and how people helped each other when she was young.

> People visit from place to place telling each other of news about what is happening in their area. No man miss [a visit of] his own relative, they go to let them know what problems they have and they can send runners to tell others what is going on. People know everything, so when people got trouble they let everyone know and they all help each other. People help each other if they get hard up for food. Relatives help each

other, all people, hand to hands one another. No person push, no person against. (Interview recorded February 1988)

This recollection of relatives helping each other, widely shared among members of the Native community, is bolstered by the close family connections of the village. In Tanacross, for example, there are twelve families tied together by blood, marriage, and sib affiliation. Of these, five families predominate, creating the core of the village structure, which is descended from one group of siblings and their affines, and representing three exogamous matrilineal sibs. Of these the Dikagiyu and Tc'a·z are said to be "related," meaning they are the same moiety, while the Naltsiin and 'Al si' dEndi' are in the opposite moiety. Because of these close relationships, the village is viewed as a "big family" (Guedon 1974: 129) that provides a network of consanguineous and affinal ties in which everyone has a place or niche ensuring both emotional and material support.

By contrast, individuals in non-Native society are believed to be isolated rather than part of a network of relationships. Non-Natives obviously have relatives; people in the village always ask me about my mine. But the Native perception is that non-Natives are less dependent on them. Thus Native people see non-Natives as cut off from their relatives and dependent on strangers whom they have to pay for any assistance. They view themselves as part of a network that is reciprocal and unstintingly generous.

Reciprocity and Generosity

Elaborated and formalized in a variety of ceremonies, ranging from communal meals to the potlatch,[15] reciprocity and generosity are fundamental principles of the Indian way. This perception was articulated by a woman who told me that to share "even down to the last piece of bread because you will get it back" was the Indian way. Reciprocity unites Native people within the same moral universe (Bently 1987: 42). Yet this unity is fissured by competition over economic resources and the difficulties in making a living on the margins of capitalism. People continue to share, but because of outside constraints and individual self-interest, they share less.

In Native culture, the most important reciprocal relationships are between members of opposite moieties. When an individual dies, his or her paternal relatives (members of the opposite moiety) build the funeral structures, act as pallbearers, and bury the body. At the subsequent potlatch, these people continue to fulfill their obligations by sharing the grief of the mourners (potlatch hosts), lifting their spirits through dance, song, and oratory, and acknowledging the status of the mourners by accepting their gifts.

In return, the mourners are obligated to compensate those who performed the funerary services and to acknowledge their status with a formal distribution of gifts. In effect, this balanced reciprocity creates an image of equality as each side becomes indebted to the other. In stark contrast is the Native view of non-Natives as having no obligation to anyone, let alone Native people. Even more vivid is their perception of a powerful and intrusive government. One of the most telling examples of this notion derives from Native people's view of their current relationship with the U.S. and Alaskan governments. People feel that in exchange for giving up much of their land and old way of life, the government has an obligation, not only to help, but to treat Native people as equal and patriotic citizens.[16] One older

woman expressed this opinion when we discussed land negotiations in which the village was involved.

> Today, forever, years ago I sign for citizen. Skip, that old man
> who came out from states, tell us good for us to sign for citizen
> and we did it because he was a friendly, kindly man and he tell
> us that the state will bring his big store and we will never be
> hard up. You going to have a better time.
>
> Now we have bad problem because someone boss for us and
> tell us what to do. If he don't bother us, don't matter where we
> want to hunt, pick berries, not fair to push one another. So
> today we belong to state, government feed us, the greatest
> help we get from government because we lose our relative, no
> father, no mother, no aunt, nobody alive with us, just a few
> people, not much people. So why now the people have to
> share with us, not push us, treat us right, share with us, not
> against us. We not against nobody. (Interview recorded
> February 1988)

As the woman says, people feel they are part of the state, but
this relationship, fraught with conflict, produces contradictory feelings in many Native people. Most people in the
village, believing that patriotism is "a good thing," express
gratitude for what the American government has done in
providing social services and protecting Alaska against Com-
munist aggression. This attitude is tempered by the realiza-
tion that Native people are discriminated against and that
they have been generally ill-treated. People see a contradiction between their feelings about America as their country
and what has happened to them. The contradiction especially
nags young people who have had some university training.

One young woman in her thirties explained, "Patriotism
is the right thing, a good thing and the people are grateful
for the government protecting them against communism."

But "there is no justice," she said, "no democracy, people are stripped of everything, their culture, their old way of life, their beliefs." She felt cheated by the American government and that her people were being pushed toward extinction. Much of the frustration Native people feel toward non-Natives is caused by their refusal to fulfill their moral obligations to treat Native people as equal. Native people point out that they not only fulfill their obligations as citizens but are themselves much more generous than non-Natives.

Native people, however, also think they were more generous in the past than they are now. This is the sentiment expressed by a man in his early sixties in an anecdote about the generosity of the hunters in times of need.

It's when I was a boy people kind of look after each other, if you got nothing to eat somebody will help you, I remember them always do that. If you run out of food somebody will always see that you're not starving. One time, around 1938, Titus Isaac family move up to Long Cabin . . . and we kill caribou whole day, lots of 'em around. But first thing old man thought about is people at Tanacross. He said we left down there, there is no fresh meat around, who had better run down there with a load, he told us.

. . . [W]e came into my daddy's house [in Tanacross] with fresh meat, sure enough they need it. . . . [I]t's all dumped in pan, in wash pan, all dump in that and clean tablecloth laid out and it cut in pieces. This family to that family. After we went [walked] thirty-five miles to get that to them it's all given away except one dog pack they kept for themselves. That's how much people think about each other. I think they really think about each other. Way up there [in the bush] that old man he remember that really good fresh meat is really needed. (Interview recorded November 1986)

Generosity, especially toward the elderly and unfortunate, was a virtue parents wanted to instill in the young. An elder relates,

> [My] mother told me don't pass poor one, don't follow that strong people, happiness people, you mistake. You see poor one, don't go by, you stop, give a little hand, give water, or something to eat then you be O.K. My mother hands go to all poor one, kid's mother die, kid's father die my mother always help them, fix their moccasin, clothe them, all that stuff momma did it. So she taught me real like that, I cannot get away, I cannot leave it, I gotta do what momma told me. (Interview recorded February 1987)

As the woman says, she was told not to follow the "strong people, happiness people," that is, people who disregard others, but to stop for the poor and unfortunate; otherwise, she would make a "mistake," meaning she could lose her good fortune. If she ignores them, they may cause her good luck to vanish by thinking about her in a malevolent way.

An obvious inference from both of these accounts is that the past was much more golden than the present, but this point of view is not mere sentiment. As a Tanacross man points out,

> People still do that [share] right now, but they use to do it a lot [more]. If you got moose today that's yours . . . when you get moose now if you give it away you just can't get another one, you know [because of the Fish and Game]. (Interview recorded November 1986)

However much generosity has declined, it remains a practical and symbolic expression of traditional values within and between villages. Today in the village, birthdays and holidays such as Christmas, New Year's, Easter, and the Fourth of July are occasions for individuals or the village as a whole to put on feasts. These festivals reinforce Native people's favorable image of themselves, and that image is enhanced when people go out of their way to help indigent non-Native people whom they meet either along the highway or in the town of Tok. In these instances, sharing becomes a symbol of superiority, in that Native people show non-Natives they are capable of great generosity, even to strangers.[17]

Although generosity, sharing, and kinship patterns are strong images of real Native life, they are considered by some people to be communistic, a label that makes many Native people, who are very patriotic, uncomfortable. The president of the village council said he did not know how he could be anti-Communist and still support some of the communal activities of the village government. He cited the example of the village laundromat, owned and operated by the village council. If the village were truly capitalist, he said, it should be run by a private operator. As if to illustrate the failure of public ownership, he pointed out that the facility is out of money and in disrepair.[18]

Love and Respect

The dual themes of "love and respect" continually appear in Native discussions about social relationships. Although love and respect are often used interchangeably, each word signifies related but still different ideals. Love is sentimental, an affection, a fondness based on personal and kinship ties. Love is also an ideal of brotherly or paternal love that may be expressed in words or a gesture. For example, if parents greatly love a child, they sew dentalium shells on the child's clothes or give the child a necklace of shells. One young man explained that when he received a beaded sash for a Christmas present, he was "bound by love" to those who had given it to him. Wearing such a sash at a potlatch is also symbolic of love and respect for one's ancestors and is considered diichaagh, something really great. One Tanacross man compared it to wearing a poppy or a flag pin on Veterans Day.

The words *love* and *respect* are also used to describe the symbolic significance of potlatch gifts. Blankets, for example, are said to be used to wrap the guest in love. As I was told several times, the potlatch is about love, love of the person for whom the potlatch is given and love for the guests. One young man went so far as to disavow any similarities between the Athapaskan potlatch and Northwest Coast potlatches of which he had read. He said there was no competition, no ostentatious giveaways as in the Northwest Coast potlatches. Instead the Athapaskan potlatch represents love and respect.[19]

Respect denotes esteem and regard for a wide range of entities, from other human beings to supernatural forces. Respect is trusting an individual to be responsible, not only to himself or herself but to all other human beings and animals (Ridington 1988: 107). An example of respect for others was the help Native people offered non-Natives during the gold rush. Tanacross people say that in 1899, a horde of gold seekers went through Tanacross territory on its way to Dawson. Native people helped many prospectors; they fed them and showed them how to prepare and cook the carcasses of moose and caribou.

Love and respect can be understood as oppositions to competition and jealousy, but they also serve as an "ideology" used to cloak competition. Sergei Kan (1986), in discussing the nineteenth-century Tlingit potlatch, has suggested that while love and respect are "basic cultural values" expressing the proper relations between moieties and the living and the dead (197), these same values serve as a rhetorical device masking competition over power and prestige (201). By couching competition in these terms, the Tlingit are able to avoid open confrontation and argument (203). Like the Tlingit, the Tanacross concept of "love and respect" expresses an ideal relationship that does not fully reflect reality. But the rhetoric is a means of mediating or avoiding conflict.[20]

While it is denied that competition exists in the potlatch, it does occur. Historically, it was enacted through potlatch oratory, public challenges, and the number of gifts distributed. In the modern potlatch, much of the overt rivalry is absent. Nevertheless, there is an underlying tension based on individual, family, village, and sib rivalry over power and prestige. To validate this prestige and gain renown, individuals and groups attempt to manipulate the potlatch to their advantage. Hosts, for instance, try to stage large and elaborate ceremonies, while guests, if they feel they have been slighted, can cause trouble by denigrating the hosts' efforts. Disagreements can also arise over such matters as etiquette (as we shall see later) or a burial. At one funeral, for example, a conflict arose over where to bury the deceased. One group wanted the body buried in one place, because the deceased was originally from that area, while others thought he should be buried in his residential village.

Competence and Incompetence

Native people regard themselves as both competent and incompetent. Competence is an integration of responsibility, knowledge, and action aimed at taking care of oneself and those dependent on one (R. Preston 1975: 274–75; S. Preston 1986: 23). In Athapaskan culture competence is differentiated by gender, and, as Julie Cruikshank (1990) so perceptively points out, this difference has implications in the modern context. In the past a woman's competence lay in her ability to apply practical, empirically based knowledge to a problem and to deal discreetly with supernatural power. Men, as hunters, by contrast, dealt directly with power, and their competence rested with their ability to seek out, use, and, if need be, challenge power (ibid., 344). Today women's practical abilities, whether as artisan or office worker, are well regarded and sought out by both Native and non-Native people. Men's ability to seek and use supernatural power, however, is not so appreciated and is considered, at best, ethereal (ibid., 345). Two areas where men can still demonstrate traditional forms of competence are the potlatch and practical skills applied to hunting.

Competency survives in people's periodic forays into the bush to hunt, trap, and fish. It is fostered by the village "4H" or "survival camp" held each summer in the old village of Mansfield where children are taught traditional forms of competence in fishing, hunting, and preparing game. Feelings of competence also come alive when the community prepares for a potlatch, but they are most vibrantly expressed in the elders' stories about the time when they were young. The following story, which I heard from Elisha, is both a nostalgic recollection of past competence and an instructive tale for the present generation. What is demonstrated in this narrative are qualities that people continue to admire and emulate: endurance, knowledge, flexibility, and confidence.

One time J., Elisha, and G.H. were out hunting around Mt. Fairplay and the little Dennison River. They spotted a moose, which J. shot, crippling it. The moose headed straight for the timber and they had to track it. All day they chased the moose, which eluded them by continually moving away even as the hunters closed in. Because the going was so rough, the men had to walk on overflow glaciers, so all day they ran after the moose dragging their snowshoes behind them. [21]

By ten o'clock that night they hadn't found the moose so they discontinued the hunt and walked over the hill to the Little Dennison where they were camped. But there was no glacier to walk on so the walking was very hard, the snow being almost waist high. By eleven o'clock J. said he was tired so they stopped to make tea, the first tea of the day. That restored them somewhat and they returned to their camp, but they had no ax. Elisha walked around and found a particular type of stump that was very hard and could be used to break firewood.

G.H. said that he had some caribou stomach left and they could cook that. This was the whole stomach lining, so they filled it with water and suspended it near the fire. The lining acted as a container that would not burn as long as it was filled with water. Elisha said that soup cooked this way was "strong" like whiskey and made them feel like they had not even walked at all. Along with the soup they ate a piece of the stomach. In the old time people sometimes carried a piece of the stomach, because, as J. said, it was good medicine, like a restorative.

The next day J. went out and encountered the moose, which had walked into a pack of wolves who had trapped it by forming a circle around it. This occurred on a lake where the wolves had been "camped" a long time. J. said that it looked as though the wolves had killed three moose by simply waiting for a moose, killing it, and living or "camping" around the kill.

When J. came upon this scene initially, all he saw was the moose lying on the ice. He gathered up a bunch of willows using them as a blind to stalk the moose. As the moose became aware of J.'s movement it got up and immediately the wolves got up, one after the other. Suddenly J. realized what was going on. He shot at the wolves, shooting first at the one that was sitting almost nose to nose with the moose, but missed. At that point the wolves started to run toward J., who fired again, killing one of the wolves. They turned and ran up into the timber on the small hills surrounding the lake. By howling and barking the wolves realized that one of their mates was missing and a big black wolf stood on top of the hill howling. J. raised his rifle and shot him in the chest.

Elisha got back to camp about eight o'clock that night and J. was not there. He made something to eat, made his bed, and prepared to sleep. At this point G.H. asked Elisha if he was going to wait for J. Elisha said no, J. would not be back until the morning and he was alright anyway, why should he wait up for J.? Sometime during the night J. came back to camp and Elisha awoke to a conversation between J. and G.H. J. had brought home a piece of meat, which they ate.

That was the end of the story.

Though the story is nostalgic, it is not sentimental. It was a "hard life," as Elisha said, and one that not many Tanacross people would like to relive. This does not mean, however, that they do not like to be out in the bush hunting or that they do not like wild food. As I have pointed out, they have made an effort to maintain the old village of Mansfield as a refuge or retreat from the world dominated by non-Natives. Like many other groups, Tanacross people feel the bush can "heal." Some villagers, for example, talk about sending drinking people up to Mansfield to dry out. In that life people knew exactly what they could and could not do. They knew what consequences their actions might have, and they took responsibility for themselves as well as others. The sense of competence this story illustrates is a legacy which equips the people, to some extent at least, to cope with the present and perhaps the future.

The story also presents an image of competence no one can dispute, providing a sustained link to the past. Yet this image is frequently overshadowed by the widespread perception, among both Natives and non-Natives, that Native people, especially men, are incompetent. This is implicit in the belief that Native people are not "strong enough" and do not know how to live their old hunting life again. It is also implied in the belief that there are no more "genuine" Natives. People condemn themselves as incompetent for not being able to maintain the old ways, but they also condemn themselves for not being able to succeed on the non-Native's economic terms. Some hold the pessimistic view that Native people are incapable of ever being successful and will eventually lose both the land and the money gained through the Alaska Native Land Claims Act. One person explained he was "not proud of Natives; they haven't gotten anywhere in the sixteen years since the land claims. If non-Natives had been in the same situation, they would have gotten somewhere."

In asserting the ideal values of the Indian way, Native people are attempting to maintain a text on what decent and seemly social relations should be. The ideal emphasizes the virtues of love and respect, generosity, reciprocity, and competence to mobilize ideas into action for the common good. These are values that link the present with the past and serve as a model for the future. They serve to maintain the distinction between Natives and non-Natives based on an opposition between the Indian way and the non-Native way. As ideals they also throw into stark contrast the contradictions that beset the reality of contemporary Native life. It is within this context that the potlatch becomes important as a point of mediation. As a representation of the ideal, or traditional Native life, participation in the potlatch is a way to maintain and reproduce what are considered to be some of the "real" aspects of Tanacross culture.

CHAPTER 6

Funerals and Preparations for an Upper Tanana River Potlatch

In Tanacross culture, there are a number of occasions on which the community draws together for purposes of celebration. But no celebration has the intensity of the death-related rituals of the funeral and potlatch. It is during this period that the community sets itself "'outside of time' in order to negotiate the premises upon which social life is based" by "recreating and communicating among themselves what they see to be the building blocks of their joint existence" (Rasnake 1988: 175).

Although intertwined, funerals and potlatches are distinct in purpose. Potlatches that follow funerals are called funeral potlatches. The potlatch marks the separation of the deceased from society and is the last public expression of grief. It is also the public acknowledgment, by the hosts, of members of the opposite moiety who fulfilled their reciprocal obligation by burying the deceased and sharing the grief. Funerals are concerned with the physical treatment of the body and entail the preparation of the corpse, the building of a coffin and the grave fence, and a Christian religious service. These may be followed by another potlatch, held at a later date, if the spouse, child, or sibling of the deceased feels one is not sufficient. These later potlatches are often called memorial potlatches. Unlike funeral potlatches, which are organized by the community under the direction of a leader, memorial potlatches are the responsibility of an individual who works to purchase the necessary food and gifts.

This chapter begins with the description of a funeral for an old woman. Within the context of her funeral, Tanacross people re-create a model of tradition that is both "real" and flexible enough to accommodate the range of individual and external forces that shape contemporary Athapaskan culture. Mediated through a combination of tradition and expediency, competition continually emerges as a dynamic spirit behind the preparations for the funeral. The remainder of the chapter concerns the preparations for a memorial potlatch held some years after the funeral. Competition again emerges as the individual host seeks to make the most lavish potlatch possible. Yet while these preparations are, initially, the responsibility of the individual, they are not simply the seed of individual rivalry but, as in the preparations for the funeral, a vehicle through which the community and the individual merge.

THE FUNERAL OF AN ELDER

The old woman died in the early hours of a winter morning surrounded by her relatives, which meant most of the people in the village. To be at her side was, as someone said, the very least they could do for "grandma."[1] Born into the Dikagiyu sib in the late 1880s, at the beginning of sustained contact with non-Natives, the old woman symbolized the history of modern Tanacross. As a reflection of her status, the village had, some years before, held a celebration in her honor.[2] At her death, the whole village again became involved, this time in preparing her funeral.

Several hours after death, the corpse was dressed by women of the opposite moiety in funeral clothes consisting of a black skirt, a white blouse, beaded moccasins, mittens, and a dentalium shell necklace. It was then wrapped in two Hudson's Bay blankets. Afterward, as tradition required, the body was removed from the house through a window to avoid the doors, which are believed to be polluted by the comings and goings of young women, and taken to the community hall. Because the hall is heated, the body was later moved to the church and a large red Bible placed next to it. Dressing the corpse immediately reaffirmed reciprocity between moieties and set a tone of cooperation for the rest of the funeral preparations.

The arrival of guests from other villages throughout the morning was also an affirmation of traditional obligation and cooperation both between villages and opposing segments of the society. The guests' first stop was the deceased's house. There they expressed condolences to the family and were welcomed with a light meal of soup, sandwiches, and coffee prepared in the house by several young women. These greetings, reflecting the occasion, were subdued but not tearful.

Just after the woman died, Jack, as a member of the opposite 'Al si' dEndi' sib, and the deceased's nephew, that is, brother's son, assumed responsibility for organizing the funeral. Jack's role was to create a sense of cooperation and facilitate activities that would lead to completion of the preparations. To this end, he collected cash donations, which he carefully counted and kept in a large roll in his front shirt pocket, and called the local office of the Alaska Department of Fish and Game for permission to kill a moose, which Alaska state law allows,[3] and then asked six or eight young men, including his eldest son, to go hunting. Since the corpse was not embalmed, Jack also had to arrange with the magistrate in Tok for the village to hold the body until the funeral. In this instance, Jack mediated the needs of the community with those of the state. By immediately acknowledging its authority, Jack indicated that the village had now met its obligation and was free to continue as tradition dictated, which is exactly what it did.

To build a consensus around his leadership and avoid another avenue of conflict, Jack visited his sibmate Elisha, the other leading man in the community. Together they discussed digging the grave and building the grave fence and coffin. They agreed to comply with the wish of the deceased to be buried next to her husband in the old graveyard across the river, though Elisha was concerned that the changing course of the river would eventually wash the cemetery away. It was also decided that anyone could help dig the grave and build the grave fence, since "this was not really old time." This decision departed from tradition because members of the opposite sib or moiety are supposed to do these things. However, Jack felt that since so many people in the village were related to the deceased, everyone should be encouraged to participate. Furthermore, by saying this was not "old time," Jack intimated this should be a community event rather than an expression of sib prerogative and prestige.

Once securing support from his sibmate, Jack contacted a local merchant, married to a Tanacross woman, for the purposes of borrowing a delivery truck to haul groceries and barrels of gasoline for the snow machines and pickup trucks used in the moose hunt. He also enlisted the man's services, and the services of his wife and children, to cook breakfast for the guests. Once these arrangements were completed, Jack took the donations he had received to Tok to purchase food, wood, and paint for the fence, tools for digging the grave, and a length of yellow plastic rope to lower the coffin into the grave. On returning to the village, Jack deposited most of the groceries in the community hall, but he gave several canned hams, coffee, mayonnaise, and bread to his older daughter so she could prepare sandwiches for the men who were building the grave fence and coffin.

After the women had prepared the corpse, the major tasks left were to build a coffin and a grave fence. For this Jack enlisted the help of his son-in-law and a local non-Native man, an expert carpenter married to a Tanacross woman. By mobilizing his own family and engaging the carpenter, Jack avoided creating tension over sib prerogative and stimulated participation by producing a situation in which people could take part on their own accord. In total, twenty-one men, mostly from Tanacross, actively participated, while men from other villages came to watch or give a hand, depending on their inclination.

Usually the immediate relatives of the deceased purchase a coffin from an undertaker in Fairbanks. On this occasion, however, the deceased had specifically asked to be buried in a homemade coffin, which is the old-fashioned way. She had stipulated a plain box, but the men lined it with a Hudson's Bay blanket and put a Pendleton "chief's" blanket on the outside to honor her. While some men worked on the coffin, others constructed the traditional fence used to mark the grave. The fence, made of lumber, was constructed in the design of a picket fence, measuring seven feet by four feet, with a cross placed at one end to mark the head of the grave. Both the cross and the tops of the pickets were cut into a decorative pattern using a hand-held electric saber saw. These decorations vary according to the gender of the individual whose grave they mark. Women's decorations are rounded; men's are pointed. After the fence was finished, it was painted green, except for the tops of the pickets, which were painted white.

Work on the coffin and fence began around 1:30 P.M. and was completed about 5:00 P.M. During construction, the atmosphere was relaxed; people talked and joked while they worked, drank coffee, and ate the ham sandwiches provided by Jack's daughter. Once the work was finished, everyone went to the community hall for supper. The meal consisted of a small quantity of moose meat, which had been donated since no moose had yet been killed, and canned fruit, tea, soup made of Spam, cabbage, potatoes, carrots, ham sandwiches, and chicken soup, which Jack had purchased earlier in Tok.

During the supper, Jack conferred with his first cousin, or "cousin sister," who was the daughter of the deceased's older brother. He told her that the coffin was finished, that it looked good, that everything went well, and that there had been a "good feeling" during the work, which meant that everything was going correctly and that people were satisfied.

The death of the old woman had created a liminal state (Turner 1974) in which daily concerns and conflicts were set aside so that the village, and the larger Athapaskan community, could draw together to restate and reaffirm both its traditional links to the past and its sense of community. Reciprocal relations between sibs of the opposite moieties had been reaffirmed at the outset with the proper treatment of the body. Competition had been negated by Jack's insistence, with Elisha's assent, that traditional sib prerogatives be set aside. Yet overlaying this sense of community was tension caused by the fact that both Jack's and the village's prestige hinged on the ability to conclude successfully the funeral preparations and to demonstrate a proper respect for the deceased and guests.

To alleviate some of this tension and to take advantage of the infusion of cash provided by the large number of visitors, a poker game began during the night and lasted until the early morning. Poker games, frequently played at funerals and potlatches, serve both as entertainment and as a way to make money. Players included people from several villages, including Tanacross. The game is always held in a private residence, for which the owners are compensated. Poker money comes from government transfer payments, wages, and cash received as a potlatch gift. On this first night, however, only those not intimately connected with the funeral played since it would be considered disrespectful to do otherwise. Or to put it another way, it might be said that someone took advantage of death to make money.

At 5:00 the following morning, two of the young men Jack had sent out hunting shot the first of four moose eventually killed for the funeral and potlatch. Before first light, they had partially butchered a cow moose. Later that morning, several of the men accompanied the hunters back to the kill to finish the butchering and bring the rest of the meat to the village. This was done at the direction of an older, more experienced man in his early forties. First, the animal was flayed and then butchered on top of the skin to prevent the meat from getting dirty. After skinning, the carcass was split into four quarters and the ribs cut away from the backbone. Because the young hunters were inexperienced, they had ruptured the stomach,

filled with undigested willows, and spilled some of the mal-
odorous contents, but luckily not on the meat. Everything,
including the skin, was carried home. Later in the day, two
more moose were killed north of the village by men hunting
on snow machines. Now that there was meat the final task was
excavating the grave.

To facilitate digging the grave, Jack had purchased three
axes and three shovels. Later, during the potlatch, these
would be given away as gifts to several of the young men of the
opposite moiety in public acknowledgment of their participation. Like the preparation of the corpse, digging the grave is
supposed to reflect the moiety structure of the indigenous
society. But in this instance, another village elder, Samuel,
who is of the Dikagiyu sib, the same sib as the deceased, took
the initiative and enlisted the help of several people including
his old friend Elisha, and a non-Native man who was a friend
of Samuel's daughter, and me.

Samuel's choice of helpers illustrates the difficulties in
organizing the village and one strategy used to surmount
them. Samuel knew that his nephews, the young men he could
rightfully ask for assistance, were unreliable because they had
been drinking. He knew others would not help because he had
no authority over them, since he was not a relative or sibmate.
Once the project got started, though, Samuel knew that
others would join on their own accord. Consequently, Samuel's initiative, rather than undermining Jack's leadership,
kept the momentum of the preparations from stalling at a
critical juncture and provided Samuel with a chance to
become involved on his own terms. Nevertheless, digging the
grave became a confused and needlessly prolonged affair.

The deceased had stipulated she wanted to be buried in the
old graveyard across the river, next to her husband and nine

children. Since few of the graves are actually marked, we spent some time looking for the site and after several hours of discussing the matter made a tentative decision. But since no one was really sure, it was decided that Elisha should go back to the village to find out exactly where to dig. After consulting with several elders, Elisha returned to say that it was all right to dig where we had chosen. So we hacked out a square in the frozen earth with the axes provided. After removing the topsoil, we started a fire using wood and old tires to thaw out the ground, but because it was getting dark, we stopped work and returned to the village, leaving the fire to burn all night. As it turned out, this was the wrong spot.

Early the following morning Elisha organized a crew of four to finish the digging. As we were shoveling out the thawed earth, Jack's son-in-law, Jim, asked if we were digging in the correct place. If we were, he said people in the village would help. This produced some acrimonious debate between Jim and the digging crew, and he apologized, saying he had not come to start trouble or cause hard feelings but only to make sure we were doing the proper thing.

Jim's question nevertheless caused considerable consternation. Some people felt that the wishes of the deceased would have to be disregarded because the funeral was the next day. A few people expressed the opinion that it would not only show disrespect but also cause bad luck, or injih, to dig in the wrong place, and they refused to dig the grave unless it was done right. To settle the confusion, Sam, the deceased's oldest nephew, showed the workers the proper site.

At this point, twelve more people became involved in digging. The composition of the work party reflected both the diversity of social relations that link the village to the outside world and the traditional aspects of participation. It included a Tlingit man, who lives with a Tanacross woman, three non-Native men, including myself, several people of mixed blood, together with a number of people from other villages. Most of the participants, however, were young men of the 'Al si' dEndi' sib encouraged by their elders, who stood by and watched the digging. Since valuable time had been lost, it was decided to dig with a chainsaw. As soon as we broke through the frozen soil, we used picks and shovels on the unfrozen earth. People attributed the ease with which we dug the grave to the fact that it was the correct place. Others also said it was easy to dig because the deceased was a good, kind person and that digging graves for mean people was very hard.

While some people worked on the grave, others cleaned up the graveyard, cutting brush and limbing trees. The old people kept a large fire going, along with a lively conversation in a mixture of the Tanacross language and English which consisted of stories and teasing by the older men of the younger men and boys. Sometimes the teasing became particularly pointed, causing confrontations that Jim smoothed over by pointing out that no insult was intended. Later in the day, Jack distributed coffee, pop, sandwiches, chewing tobacco, and cigarettes when he came out to check on the progress of the excavation.

The significance of caring for the corpse, building the grave fence and coffin, and excavating the grave is tied to how a person's identity is carried forward in time. As the oldest member of the community, the old woman represented the generation responsible for producing and nurturing all the present generations of Tanacross people. Her identity was carried forward in the grief of those whom she "held" or nurtured. To become involved in preparing her funeral was to honor and increase her value, not only as a human being but as a person responsible for the lives of all those still living. By linking themselves to the deceased, and hence all her generation, through the labor of the funeral, Tanacross people were able to formulate and re-create their shared identity. Through these expressions of mutual concern and care, of love and respect, they also reaffirmed their identity in contrast to what they see as a fragmented and individualistic non-Native society. By laboring for others in a community effort rather than for oneself, they endeavor to maintain their wholeness as human beings.

Placing the grave in the appropriate place was a matter of demonstrating respect for the deceased and affirming social links between the past and present. It was also a matter of prestige. Responsibility for successfully carrying out the deceased's wishes lay, ultimately, with Jack and members of the opposite sib. To avoid criticism and to validate his position as a tradition bearer, Jack was bound to carry out the deceased's request. Furthermore, because the deceased was his paternal aunt, Jack felt a personal obligation, since in honoring the deceased he also honored his father and his father's sib.

Not all situations were so neatly resolved. At one point, Elisha and Samuel had a discussion about one young man, a non-Athapaskan who had contributed both his labor and a moose to the funeral. Because the young man lived with his niece, Elisha had an interest in whether he would be compensated. But apart from a personal interest, Elisha also believed it was the correct thing to do. He therefore suggested that the worker should be "paid" or rewarded with a potlatch gift for his considerable contribution. This was, after all, the responsibility of the Dikagiyu, since the deceased was their relative, and Samuel agreed.

As a Dikagiyu elder, Samuel was theoretically the leading man for all the Dikagiyu in the village. Traditionally, this would mean that under his direction these people would participate and provide some gifts for the subsequent pot-latch, thus enhancing Samuel's prestige as a leader. But Samuel is self-effacing and not a particularly dynamic leader. Furthermore, family ties take precedence over sib affiliation, and since the deceased was a member of Jack's family, he could be pivotal in influencing the distribution of gifts. In the end the young man never received a gift, and it was rumored that someone had manipulated the distribution of the gifts to his disadvantage. In fact, this situation eventually produced criti-cism because several people, including Lila, Elisha's wife and an important Dikagiyu woman, felt the young man and a number of other people were inappropriately compensated for their contributions. This is exactly the kind of criticism to be avoided because it diminishes the value of the potlatch and the prestige of those who give it and those for whom it is given.

This incident illustrates two points. First, while coopera-tion is essential for completing the preparations, it does not obviate the underlying competitive tensions between various segments of the community. Second, the increasing involve-ment of non-Athapaskans leads to ambiguous situations that are actively exploited to the advantage of different potlatch participants. In this instance, the young man made a substan-tial contribution that was ignored.

To this point, the preparations for the funeral had been led exclusively by the Native community. The funeral service was, however, entrusted to the local Episcopal priest, assisted by a Native Christian fundamentalist minis-ter from Copper Center and a local Wycliffe Bible transla-tor fluent in the Upper Tanana language. It was held in the community hall because the church was simply not big

enough to accommodate the assembly. To transform the hall
for the service, a cross and candles were brought over from the
church. Then, just before the service, someone hung up long
pieces of cloth, which covered a large portion of the walls and
several windows. Asked why this was done, several people
gave various answers. One said that different families had
different magic or medicine, while another said it was a partial
display of what would be given away at the potlatch later that
evening. A third person, when asked if it had anything to do
with magic, answered with studied indifference. Later, after
the funeral, the cloth was torn off the wall and used in the
dancing and singing as a signal that the mourning period had
ended.

During the funeral, the mourners sat on church benches
and folding chairs set out in rows facing a dais and table. The
coffin was placed on the table diagonally across the room
separating the congregation from the officiants. On top of the
coffin were several arrangements of plastic flowers. The Native fundamentalist minister from Copper Center started the
service with a prayer in English. He was followed by the
Episcopal priest, who read the liturgy, also in English. Then
the Wycliffe translator sang two songs and read from the Bible
in the Upper Tanana language. The service was concluded by
the Episcopal priest, at which time the congregation filed past
the open casket to pay its last respects. Then the pallbearers,
men from the opposite moiety, hauled the coffin on a sled to
the grave.

Those who had relatives in the cemetery, one of three
located near the old village, brushed snow off the grave houses
and generally tidied up the area. The Episcopal priest and the
Wycliffe translator read the burial service. Then the coffin
was lowered into the grave with yellow plastic rope, and in a

final act of respect each person present threw in a handful of dirt. Finally, the grave was filled in and the grave fence set so that it was level with surrounding graves.

Christian funeral services have become a vital part of traditional Tanacross mortuary ritual practice. Native people believe they need a non-Native priest to interpret Christianity correctly, and they tend to view the Christian burial service as a sign of equal status with non-Natives. As one Tanacross man put it, Christianity is like being "civilized." In this respect, the service should emulate as closely as possible a non-Native funeral with cross, candles, and flowers. Also, the dress of the participants, especially the deceased's relatives, should correspond to that worn at a non-Native middle-class funeral. And the mourning should be subdued. Thus the service underlines the fundamental idea of the equality of Native and non-Native, based not only on the overarching concept of universal Christian love but also on the shared ritual legitimized by the presence of the priest.

The reverence for the authority of the Episcopal Church is based on the deep respect felt for the elders who first accepted the Church. One important facet of this acceptance was the attractive concept of an afterlife. Old people today talk about their relief when learning from the missionaries that becoming a Christian meant being reunited with relatives in heaven. In this context the meaning of the service has been reformulated to express the importance of cross-generational kinship ties or the unity of generations, which is also one aspect of the potlatch. Displaying the long bolts of cloth served to bridge the funeral to the subsequent potlatch, binding the mourners in the common purpose of honoring the deceased and by extension all her generation. This was further emphasized by Jack, who wore, over his blue suit, a wide beaded sash that, like the cloth on the walls, was a statement of honor for the deceased.

As we have seen, the death of an individual involves the total community. The tension between tradition and expediency, between personal and group goals, that characterized the funeral is also evident in preparations for a memorial potlatch that may be held years after a funeral. What is different is that these arrangements, initially, do not involve the whole community, but social pressures and the economics of modern potlatches dictate that individuals eventually accommodate themselves to the group. Nevertheless, memorial potlatches remain intensely personal commitments. The individual's goal is to prepare the largest and most lavish ceremony possible because it demonstrates his or her feelings for the deceased and adds to his or her personal standing in the community.

PREPARATIONS FOR A MEMORIAL POTLATCH

During the 1980s, a woman named Helen made a memorial potlatch for her son who had died of cancer several years before. At first, her preparations were semisecret, since she wanted no help. She told me that she had literally starved herself to save money for the gifts. In the meantime, she had purchased all of the gifts and food she could afford and had finished all the beadwork she planned to give away. But she alone did not have the resources to feed all the guests over a two- or three-day period. It was therefore essential that she make some arrangement to share expenses for the feasts.

Helen arranged to share expenses with her granddaughter, Lucy, who planned a potlatch in memory of her daughter. By combining efforts, both women hoped, initially, to make the potlatch a family event. In this way, the prestige derived from a successfully staged potlatch would not have to be shared. However, because of the lack of resources, they agreed to combine efforts with two other women. Suzie, a young woman in her early thirties, was preparing a potlatch to commemorate the recovery of her brother from a serious accident. Like Helen, she had told no one outside her immediate family of her plans, but had accumulated a variety of gifts and food. Suzie's major support came from her mother, a very knowledgeable elder, who assisted her by making several gifts. The third person to join Helen was Jean, a woman in her early sixties, who was preparing a potlatch for three different people, including two little boys, not her sons, who had caught their first fish.

While family considerations play a primary role in the organization and preparation of potlatches, an important consideration in combining efforts is sib solidarity. We saw this when Jack made it a point to consult with Elisha and when he consulted with his "cousin sister," or first cousin, about the progress of preparations for the funeral. In the case of Helen's potlatch, all of the women were members of the Naltsiin/'Al si' dEndi' sib. By collaborating, the women could stage a much larger and more elaborate ceremony, enhancing not only their individual prestige but the prestige of their sib as well. This consideration had prompted some villagers to say that only people in the same sib should make potlatches together, but others expressed the opinion that it was better for opposite sibs to combine. That way, the competition between sibs was minimized and the distribution of gifts was more balanced as everyone got something.

Family and sib linkages are the basis for social action within the village, but successful action requires a wider network of support. In preparing for the funeral potlatch, we saw that Jack mobilized a wide range of people, both Native and non-Native, village resident and nonresident. While Helen's network was not as extensive as Jack's, she was able to mobilize a diversity of people, including me and my research assistant. The two of us cooked a turkey for her and helped serve food during the feast. In similar fashion, Lucy, Helen's daughter, asked for assistance from various people. She had decided that to honor her daughter properly she should have her grave fence rebuilt by the non-Native carpenter and an unrelated friend. Once the project got started, others joined, including Elisha, Jack, Samuel, and me. Additionally, through-out the actual ceremony Jack assisted the hosts by encouraging Helen's grandsons to drum and sing. It was this type of assistance, coupled with the host's prodigious efforts, that made the potlatch a success. The wide range of participation transformed Helen's efforts into a community event. As the need arose, more people became involved. Some opened their houses to the guests for a place to stay, others cooked food, and still others helped clean the community hall. Thus Helen's potlatch had become an opportunity for the village to en-hance its image as a hospitable and traditionally able commu-nity. While this was a community objective, the potlatch essentially remained an individual endeavor in which prestige and satisfaction would fall ultimately to the four women who had made the primary investment.

In economic terms, potlatches require considerable invest-ment. Most money comes from wages, government transfer payments,[4] and donations. However, none of these sources of income alone is sufficient to cover the cost of a potlatch.[5] Helen, for example, is employed part-time throughout the year, as is Jean. Suzie works full-time. Helen's granddaughter and husband are both seasonally employed. All receive various transfer payments. Although each had other financial commitments, such as car payments and utility bills, all of them, like most Native people living in the bush, own their homes outright, which leaves an undetermined amount of their cash as potential surplus for the potlatch. Nevertheless, as noted above, the preparation for a memorial potlatch requires considerable personal sacrifice.

Among the many expenses, the largest are guns, blankets, and food. For purchasing the major gifts of guns and blankets, a host has two options. The first is to buy everything from retail outlets. The second is to purchase some of the guns and blankets from relatives and others who may want to sell some of the gifts they have received at potlatches. Although Helen had the option of purchasing guns from her relatives for a cost of $150 each, she chose to purchase all seventeen of her guns in Tok at a cost of $200 each, a special price given her by the proprietor of the local sporting goods store. When asked why she did this, instead of buying from friends and relatives, she said she did not want to pay the cheaper price as she loved her son so much.[6]

Although Helen insisted on purchasing new guns, she did buy used blankets at potlatches for a cost of $10 each. She also distributed a number of beaded items, including woven beaded sashes and various kinds of necklaces, which she made herself. In addition, she purchased a quantity of food including several turkeys, cases of soda, cases of vegetables, flour, sugar, tea, cases of fruit, and two beaver carcasses that she served to the elders. As with the beadwork, the beaver served to create an image of a richer ceremony, especially since beaver meat is seldom served at potlatches.

Though I have no exact figures for Helen's potlatch, I can estimate the cost. Her biggest expenditure was for the 17 rifles, which, at $200 each, cost a total of $3,400. She distributed 175 blankets at an average cost of $10 each, for a total of $1,750. Together these items cost Helen $5,150. This figure does not include the cost of the food or labor in making the beadwork or the materials or the cash distributed. Helen and her three co-hosts distributed 550 blankets, for a total of $5,500, and 40 guns, at an average cost of $175 each, for a total of $7,000. In aggregate these gifts cost $12,500.

This cost compares with two funeral potlatches for which I have figures. At the funeral potlatch for the elder Tanacross woman, held earlier in 1987, 40 guns, worth $7,000, were distributed, as well as 600 blankets, for a total of $13,000.[7] This excludes the food, which included portions of four moose, the gas provided for the hunt, and the cash given away. I would estimate that the total cost of this potlatch came to $15,000. For a funeral potlatch held on the Copper River in December 1986, the hosts spent $4,800 for food and cash gifts. They distributed 41 guns at an average price of $225, for a total of $9,225.[8] In addition, 705 blankets were distributed, totaling $7,050. The cost of this potlatch was $21,075.

The costs of the two funeral potlatches represent an aggregate of donations made by people from a number of different villages. In the potlatch held on the Copper River, the cost also included a monetary donation made by Ahtna Incorporated, the regional Native corporation. Donations for the potlatch that followed the older Tanacross woman's funeral came from both the host group or members of the moiety of the deceased and the guest group or members of the moiety opposite the deceased. The host group donations represent moiety solidarity made in honor of the deceased to assist the mourners in making a successful potlatch. Such assistance is usually rendered in blankets, guns, and cash. Donations from the guest group, in contrast, are always made in cash and meant to maintain social linkages between villages and non-related people. Cash eliminates the possibility that a guest might receive his own gift and allows the host to make use of the donation anonymously, thus maintaining the host-guest relationship. All donations made at a funeral potlatch are recorded by the host and publicly acknowledged just prior to the distribution. No such acknowledgments are necessary at a memorial potlatch since there is no donation, except in labor, which is often acknowledged through the distribution of the gifts.

Given the seeming preoccupation with accumulating gifts, some scholars have argued that the potlatch has been reduced to an exhibition of individual aggrandizement characteristic of a market economy. In Tanacross, however, external economic forces have not transformed the potlatch into an arena for individual rivalry but have led to the maintenance of social relations as individuals seek to cooperate in order to potlatch. I do not mean that individual achievement goes unrecognized but that such endeavors are not simply defined by the market economy. In the funeral, for example, each individual contribution is noted and publicly acknowledged, but it is the totality of the group's effort that has most significance. Similarly, while memorial potlatches are the result of individual accomplishment, they are transformed by village participation into collective expressions of group identity.

In the context of the funeral and preparing for a memorial potlatch, we have looked at two sets of relationships: those that create linkages within the village and those that link the village to the larger world. In the case of the funeral, the discussion centered on the leader's attempts to mobilize the community in a ceremony befitting both the deceased and the village. By reaffirming relationships, securing a consensus on his leadership, and creating noncompetitive situations, he mediated competition between sibs and families. In the case of the memorial potlatch, the four women joined in a cooperative effort to defray its costs and to stage a ceremony that would honor the participants. In both cases, however, competition was a motivating factor, since both individual and village prestige hinged on the ability to demonstrate respect for the deceased and competence in carrying out tradition.

The funeral and preparations for the memorial potlatch became a blend of tradition and improvisation. The traditional linkages between opposite moieties were reaffirmed in the funeral when women of the opposite moiety took care of the corpse. However, everyone was allowed to help prepare the grave fence, coffin, and grave to accommodate the diversity of the village population, including non-Natives. The participation of the Christian ministers legitimized the funeral service and reflected the close relationship between the Church and the community, while respectful participation of non-Natives in general re-created the image of social relations between Native and non-Native as Natives believe they should be. These same linkages present in the funeral and preparations for the memorial potlatch are maintained and formalized through the sequence of events that make up the potlatch, which is the subject of the next chapter.

Charlie James dressed for a potlatch at Tetlin, 1981. His vest is made of hand-tanned moose skin. Over the vest he is wearing two bandoliers, one made of beads and one made of Japanese dentalium shells. His headband is beaded.

An evening feast at a Tanacross potlatch, 1981.

Ahtna, Upper Tanana, and Tanacross men warming up for a dance at a Tanacross potlatch, 1987.

Tanacross children in their dance costumes at a Tanacross potlatch, 1987.

Dancers with *gunhos,* or dance sticks, at a Tanacross potlatch, 1973. The guns hanging on the wall in the background will be given away the next evening. In the upper left-hand corner is a a five-pointed star, a potlatch sign that is a symbol for the Dikagiyu sib.

Singing the Xwtiitl ch'itiik, or giveaway song, at a Tanacross
potlatch, 1987.

Joe Joseph, dressed in his chief's coat and antique dentalium shell necklace, at a Tanacross potlatch, 1972.

CHAPTER 7

Rituals of the Upper Tanana River Potlatch

The descriptions in this chapter are drawn from three potlatches I attended at different times during the late 1980s. Two were funeral potlatches held at the death of elderly women. The first of these was held in the Ahtna village of Chistochina; the second, which I discussed in chapter 6, was held in Tanacross. The third ceremony was the memorial potlatch held by Helen and her three co-hosts at Tanacross, also discussed in chapter 6.

THE HALL

All potlatches are held in a community hall that serves not only as a "potlatch house" but also as a bingo hall and a site for the community Christmas party as well as various feasts and funerals. The community hall is a large, well-lighted, centrally heated building, well suited for a potlatch. The Tanacross community hall has five rooms: a main hall, approximately seventy-five feet long by thirty feet wide, a storage room, a kitchen, and two bathrooms. On one wall of the main room are color portraits of village elders who, photographed in ceremonial regalia, stand as icons to tradition. In a similar vein, a woodcut, provided by the Tanana Chiefs Conference, depicts a group of men dressed in skin chief's coats. These are the original Tanana chiefs who began negotiations with the government over land in the early 1900s. The outcome of their efforts is symbolized by the American flag and two red, white, and blue dance sticks hanging on an opposite wall. Together, these represent the rights, equality, and power vested in citizenship that Native people demand in their quest to determine their own destiny.

This quest is reflected in the montage of black-and-white photographs of the Tanacross dogsled race that hangs on another wall. The photographs illustrate Native participation in a sport that has brought some prosperity and statewide recognition and a sense of pride to Native people. At the far end of the hall, pushed up against the wall, is the bingo paraphernalia. Both the dogsled race photographs and the bingo equipment represent the diversions of modern Native life. What is troubling to men like Elisha is that these diversions now share the same physical space with the potlatch, which reinforces his feeling that the ceremony has become trivialized or commercialized.

FEASTING

Sharing food is an important vehicle for expressing social relationships. It communicates sentiment, affection, familiarity, and goodwill. Through the feast the host creates an impression of an endless supply of food, an expression of his love and respect for the guests. Since the guests are the host's paternal relatives and potential affines, feeding them becomes a demonstration of affection for the host's father and of goodwill toward possible marriage partners. Additionally, by feeding his potential affines, the host symbolically nourishes future generations. By distributing more food than anyone could possibly eat, the host demonstrates his competence, and the surplus, which people carry home, is a reminder of the host's generosity long after the event.[1]

Wild food is preferred to most purchased foods, and it is also symbolic of Indianness. Moose meat especially symbolizes rights to land and the management of local resources based on cultural imperatives. In speeches made by the elders, wild food is often referred to as "our food." For Tanacross people, killing a moose and eating its meat is a reiteration of their traditional hunting life and of individual competence and autonomy. The success of a communal meal or potlatch is measured in large part by the amount of moose meat served. In Tetlin, for instance, Libby Halpin (1985: 34) observes that "moose meat is coveted" and that "a real meal is only one with wild food, particularly wild meat."

Although wild food is central to a potlatch feast, strong black tea, pilot bread (a form of cracker), and bannock (a form of unleavened bread) have been incorporated as traditional fare. This menu, reflecting the diet of the traditional culture of the 1920s and 1930s,[2] is always supplemented by a wide variety of store food that includes bread, canned ham, carrots, frozen chicken, potatoes, prepared meats, rice, spaghetti, and Spam, all of which are purchased in Tok or Fairbanks. At every potlatch a breakfast of fried eggs, bacon, ham, Spam, potatoes, coffee, and tea is prepared and served each morning in the community hall. The lunch menu consists of sandwiches, soup, occasionally wild meat, and tea. During the evening feasts, all the guests are served a diversity of food ranging from moose head soup to spaghetti. Food for these evening feasts is prepared in the community hall, out-of-doors, and in people's houses. The host along with his relations and friends all join in the preparation. Women cook such food as doughnuts, ham, turkey, and salads. Men between the ages of about twenty and forty-five gather to spend the whole day socializing, butchering, and cooking meat outside, especially in the summer. They separate the meat into piles for frying and boiling. They empty the boiling meat and bones into large pots of water placed over a wood fire. After the meat becomes tender, they add packets of soup mix along with rice, turnips, and various other raw vegetables. The moose head, the most traditional of food and considered the pièce de résistance of any potlatch, is also cooked this way.

The evening feasts are the most important meals served at a potlatch, and, depending on the circumstances, they are attended by between 100 and 250 people who are all fed at the same time. If the host and deceased are important, highly regarded persons, the potlatch will be well attended and all the guests, regardless of age, join in the evening feast. Most residents from the host village also attend, but there are always some people who stay away because they are drinking or because of shyness or lack of interest. It is difficult to estimate the number or gender of people who do stay away. Most often it is the young men, between the ages of twenty and forty-five, who prefer to watch television or visit with friends. Many of these same people are nevertheless involved in some aspect of the preparation.

In villages on the upper Tanana River, the evening feast is served on long strips of paper rolled out on the floor. This is considered the "traditional" way and marks the evening feast from other communal meals that are served on tables. After the paper has been put down, young men and women hand out tin cans filled with sugar, salt and pepper shakers, plates, knives, forks, and Styrofoam cups. At Tanacross, food served at a potlatch is usually eaten off crockery rather than plastic plates. Since the evening feast is communal, it is scheduled for a specific time, as opposed to breakfast and lunch, which are served over the course of several hours so that people may eat when they wish. The significance of the evening feast is also reflected in the large variety of wild food served, including beaver, mountain squirrel, duck, and moose head soup, and by the fact that it is always blessed with a Christian prayer led by a local minister or lay person. Although moose meat may be served at breakfast and lunch, these meals are usually limited to several kinds of commercial food.

In Tanacross, the host's family and friends serve the food from large containers carried up and down the rows of guests. The fact that young women now serve and cook food is a major departure from tradition. Historically, it was considered *injih* or bad luck, for pubescent women to have anything to do with food served to men. The task was left to young men and older women. The change is frequently commented on by older people, who feel this breach in tradition is just one example of the breakdown in the traditional moral order.

In the past the men ate first while the women and children were left to pick up the leavings (McKennan 1959: 136). Today everyone eats at the same time. A guest's status is reflected both in the seating arrangement and in the order of serving the food. Village elders and middle-aged guests sit on benches and chairs along the walls; young men and women and children sit on the floor in the middle of the hall. Old people are always served first. Service usually begins with huge pots of strong tea. If the hosts are slow in serving it, some guests may start singing "We want tea." Following the tea, moose meat contained in cardboard boxes is served to the elders, who pick through the boxes for a fat, meaty piece. Next come pans of fried moose meat, boxes of dried or roasted muskrat, boiled duck, pans of Copper River salmon, a variety of salads, pilot bread, baked bread, sandwiches, Styrofoam cups of blueberries, cranberries, and Jello, plastic bowls of moose head soup, fried chicken, and pans of spaghetti. Unless there is enough wild food to go around, the children receive only store-bought food, particularly spaghetti, which is considered "kids food." By the end of the feast, the elders' plates are piled high with food, which is wrapped in aluminum foil and stuffed into plastic bags to take home. On the final night of any potlatch, all of the store food and cooked wild food is given away. After everyone finishes eating, the now-soiled paper is rolled up along with all of the empty paper plates and cups, and the floor is swept and mopped. At this point there is a lull in the activity as people take their excess food out of the hall to their houses, cars, or lodgings.

DANCING AND SINGING

During one potlatch at Tanacross, after the evening feast was completed, several leading men sat in the corner of the hall quietly talking and occasionally spitting a stream of tobacco juice into a Coke can or Styrofoam cup. After about fifteen or twenty minutes, one of the old men from the village mischievously complained aloud that the hosts were "stingy for a drum" and that he should go off and get his own. Ignoring him, the men continued to wait until two young women each brought in a drum and laid it on the floor, whereupon each was picked up by two of the men. Lightly tapping the drum heads, checking to see if they are tight, the men began to warm up their voices. Finally, as they found a common tune, they, and all the men around them, burst into song.

Singing and dancing are always accompanied by the drum called Ch'elxal, which is a tambourine variety made of moose skin stretched over a birch frame. Not everyone has the ability or predilection to be a good drummer, and the importance attached to a man's ability to drum and lead songs is reflected in what people say about the drum. As one man said, "It leads the potlatch," that is, it is like an important person, and like a person, "makes noise . . . and good news in the dance." The sound of the drum is compared to a leading man making a congenial speech for "good favor and good feeling." Its reverberations make people "feel friendly" and enable them to have a "good time." Without the drum, "it does not look [or feel] like a good time." The drum reminds people of the importance of potlatch, and when people hear the drum, they know something important is going on.

Since the drum is so important, there are rules pertaining to its use. Only men are supposed to pick up the drum, but now young women will occasionally use the drum during less formal occasions. It is said that only men who have led a good clean life can use the drum, which has to be treated "right"; one cannot "rush with it." The drum has power to arouse people's emotions. To abuse that power by hurrying means that if the drummer makes mistakes, he can upset the harmony he endeavors to create through his drumming. Dancing, or Ch'uuljus, and singing, or Ch'eedutiigidiyaa, are integral to the potlatch. At funeral potlatches, songs are sung in a particular sequence beginning with "sorry songs," followed by "dance songs" and much later by a "potlatch song" sung over the gifts immediately prior to distribution. At a memorial potlatch, the same sequence is followed, except there is less emphasis on singing sorry songs. If the potlatch is entirely concerned with celebration, the sorry songs are omitted. The terms "sorry song" and "dance song" refer to dancing and singing done together, while potlatch songs are sung standing still.

Generally speaking, dancing and singing are part of the reciprocal obligation fulfilled by the guests. In exchange for food and gifts, the guests are expected to sing for the hosts both as entertainment and as a way of support in mourning and to have a good time. In fact, dancing is so important that outstanding dancers are singled out and given potlatch gifts. Guests from different villages compete with each other and with their hosts to prove themselves the best dancers.

No one is "supposed to hang back" from dancing. Guests are expected to dance hard because the movement of the dance helps to "break out the good time." That is why people say that to dance at someone's potlatch is to do "a favor for the hosts."[3] Through intense dancing, visitors are said to "accomplish" something and satisfy both themselves and their hosts. This is particularly important at funerals, where guests are expected to lift the spirits of the mourners by "breaking out the good time" and loosening up the bad luck, which would otherwise remain with one.[4]

Sorry songs eulogize the dead. They vary in intensity, depending on the circumstances of death and the feelings of the composer. Because grief is a particularly powerful emotion, somewhat independent of human will, it has to be physically expelled from a person's mind and body before it becomes unhealthy.[5] The structure of the song and accompanying dance provides for such release. Each sorry song creates an image of the deceased and arouses feelings of loneliness and loss. Repeated over and over, the lament is interspersed with a chant.[6] As the mourners sing, they pull their arms away from the body to the rhythm of the drum in an attempt to pull the grief out. At times this action is reduced to an up-and-down motion of the hands dramatizing a sense of fretting. In circumstances when the pain is particularly intense, other dancers gather close by the mourners in physical support.

To expel their grief, mourners used to dance and sing for days on end; now dancing is limited to three days. At a funeral potlatch, the mourning process begins with a sorry song made expressly for the deceased. During this first song only the hosts and the relatives of the deceased dance. This initial dance expresses sib solidarity by distinguishing the mourners from the guests. Following this song, all the guests join in, and a succession of different sorry songs are sung, punctuated by an occasional dance song. In singing a series of sorry songs, close relatives of the guests are reminded of their own loss, which enables them to empathize with the emotions of the hosts.

At one potlatch in Tanacross, for example, a sequence of sorry songs began with one made especially for the person who had just died. It was followed by songs for a young man who had died in a house fire ten years before, for a boy who drowned in the river while attempting to draw water, and for Elisha's father, who died in the 1960s. [7] The song for the person who had just died was made by William, one of the few remaining song makers in the Upper Tanana Region. Sorry songs are composed with reference both to a particular quality of the deceased and to some "lonely" sound such as a church bell or a riverboat whistle. A sorry song for Chief Isaac, for example, was made to the sound of the latter. The first sorry songs establish a common relationship among the potlatch participants based on shared grief. Each succeeding song extends the grief back in time, drawing together both the living and the dead. Like sharing the labor of digging the grave and building the coffin, grieving becomes a way of re-creating social links between generations and enabling hosts and guests to express their shared identity. Some people break down during the dancing because "they understood what the song meant." By choosing the songs, the lead singers are able to control the grieving process, keeping it within socially acceptable bounds. As one person put it, the mourners "sing WU WU back and forth, singing the sadness away and then out comes the calico!"

The mourners' mood is expected to change when they dance joyfully with long strips of calico, which are a sign of a good time. Dance songs are joyful, loud, and playful and are sung whenever people feel like dancing.[8] Bodily move-ments accompanying dance songs are flamboyant, partic-ularly for the men. Their feet planted wide apart and holding either a scarf or pieces of toweling or tissue paper, the men jab the air to the beat of the drum. They sing about familiar topics, including the village of Tanacross, the dangerous business of fighting forest fires, the beautiful women of Northway, and driving to Fairbanks. This last is based on the sound of a running automobile (Guedon 1974: 222). The excitement and anticipation of now-mundane events, like driving to Fairbanks, are recalled and famil-iarized, as are non-Native holidays such as Christmas and New Year's. The dangerous business of fighting forest fires, considered an especially traditional form of Native wage labor, is further incorporated into tradition when the exhil-aration produced by the danger of the fire is shared and reexperienced in the context of the potlatch. Women form a circle around the men and either stand still while moving their arms or dance in a shuffling counter-clockwise movement. They often playfully pull men onto the dance floor at the same time. To keep the dancing going, the drummers and lead singers sing one song after another until they are exhausted.

Because singing and dancing are so integral, not only to the potlatch, but to Native cultural expression, adults make an effort to encourage the children to participate. On special occasions the young people of the host village often dance for the guests. At the old woman's potlatch, for example, the evening ceremonies began with the arrival of a group of young people called the Tanacross Singers who paraded into the hall dressed in their felt dance costumes, beaded moccasins, headbands, and beaded sashes. Cloth dance costumes were developed in the late 1960s and adopted by the Tanacross children at the suggestion of the local schoolteacher. The first felt costumes were made in colors symbolizing the sib of the child. Red and white stood for the Dikagiyu, Tc'a·z, and Tcicyu sibs, while black and white stood for the Naltsiin and black and gold stood for the 'Al si' dEndi'.[9] The colors of the costumes have been changed to purple and white, signifying village rather than sib affiliation. Chosen because they were close to the purple and gold of the softball team called the Tanacross Chiefs, the new colors indicate that sib affiliation is giving way to a village-oriented structure, in part because fewer and fewer people, particularly the young people, know which sib they belong to.[10]

The children, joined by a few adults who supported their sometimes wavering voices, sang about Tanacross. Soon more and more people joined in until the hall vibrated. Now people shoved and pushed, laughed and shouted, as dancers began pulling one another onto the floor. Children, men, and women all danced to one song after another. People yipped and trilled their voices. They pulled down strips of cloth tacked up on the walls, each grabbing a section to form a chain of dancers that moved counterclockwise. After several songs, they ripped the strips of cloth into sections to be given away later as gifts. As the crowd in the center of the hall swelled, the intensity of the dancing and singing grew. The dancing ended when the exhausted adults had to sit down. During the lull, some people went outside to cool off in the subzero temperatures or to relieve themselves. All of the dancers sipped cans of cold pop.

The last type of song sung at all funeral and memorial potlatches is the Xwtiitl ch'itiik, or "giveaway song,"[11] more commonly called the "potlatch song." Intimately connected with the gifts, the song is sung just before distributing them. It is sung by the potlatch hosts, supported in the singing by sib leaders, who are strong singers and know the song very well. The rhythm and beat of the potlatch song is very distinct from both sorry songs and dance songs. Although the songs are personal, that is, made for a specific person, they have a general intent to spiritualize the gifts so that they will bring good luck to the host and convey the appropriate feelings. The song has to be sung precisely, without faltering or making mistakes, since it is considered injih to make a mistake (Guedon 1974: 220). It is to be sung only three times; otherwise, the luck will go too far out and may not come back. When the song is sung, it is sent out or "travels" and then comes back.

Through their combined effort, the singers alleviate the mourner's grief, eradicate bad or negative feelings, and spiritualize the gifts so that they become complete demonstrations of the host's feelings and intent "so people won't miss that person."

ORATORY

At all potlatches public speeches are a vital part of the reciprocal obligation each side, guests and hosts, must fulfill. Speeches can be loosely categorized into four types: condolence speeches, etiquette speeches, homilies delivered by elders to the young, and gratitude speeches. Condolences, often delivered formally, are offered by the guests to the hosts, and gratitude speeches, accorded to the guests by the host, are often exchanged, each side using expressions of love and respect that strengthen "good favor and good feeling" among the participants. This harmony is occasionally broken by speeches criticizing the behavior of either the guests or the hosts. Like the first two types, these speeches, traded back and forth, illustrate the competition between sibs and moieties over power and prestige. Often an elder will address a homily to the participants urging the young people to follow the Indian way. These speeches are frequently delivered informally and in a mixture of Athapaskan and English, separating them from the very formal oratory of the old men delivered in a very particular style.

Condolence speeches are often delivered formally using genealogical references and metaphors that require considerable knowledge, which, in the past, was limited to those of high rank. Today this knowledge is limited to a few elders. One relatively well understood metaphor, currently still used in condolence speeches, invokes the sacred hills and mountains connected to each major village along the Tanana and Copper river valleys.[12] The people of Tanacross, for example, have two such places: Na Dain xoo and the smaller Mesiintsits'ii'. Below, a Tanacross elder talks about the importance of these places and how he learned about them.

All through my young life.
I heard my grandpas speak of Na Dain xoo and Mesiintsits'ii'.
This too is used.
And the two were kept together and used together for
    important issues.
By my grandfathers.
Those two places were valued very high by people from all
    over the Country too.
People who were not in the high important category did not
    talk or mention those places.
Only smart wise old people did . . . and only those leaders
talked about Na Dain xoo and Mesiintsits'ii'.
Only them, no one else.
Our grandmothers, aunts and uncles and especially the
    grandmothers who were married to those great men.
Learned and remembered.
So they could pass the information on to their children.[13]

Each "important place" connects the land to the people and
their ancestors. It also symbolizes the moral strength and
physical endurance of the "top men" of each sib. In continuing to live literally beneath these named places, the people are
said to be continually reminded of the power of these men
whom they should strive to emulate. In memory, the old men,
the "grandfathers," are still alive, are "still there," and when
people speak about the hill, it is as though they "call Great-
Grandpa and Hill in the same time" (Guedon 1974: 147).

To explain the importance of Na Dain xoo, people say that
the hill is just like an American flag and has the same
importance. One man, for example, remembers how he used
to watch the flag ceremony at the military base once located
near the village and how the soldiers' respect for the flag was
similar to the people's respect for Na Dain xoo. In this way,
people explain that the rocky spire of Na Dain xoo stands for

more people and is greater than the small hill of Mes-iintsits'ii', which he compares to the Alaska state flag. This suggests that Mesiintsits'ii' stands for one sib while Na Dain xoo symbolizes the intermoiety marriages between the two most influential sibs in the Tanacross area: the Dikagiyu and the Naltsiin/'Al si' dEndi'.

At a funeral potlatch held in a Copper River village, a senior headman offered condolences to the hostess, who had just lost her sister. Walking to the middle of the floor, he stood directly in front of her. In the Upper Tanana language, he said, and I paraphrase, "Don't make yourself too cheap by grieving deeply for your beloved sister. You come from di-ichaagh, people who are really great. I know who these people are." As he spoke he pointed to Mount Sanford, the 14,000-foot volcano that symbolizes the ranking men of the de-ceased's sib. He continued, "Your people were so great that you do not have to feel bad, and you should remember not to let your grief get you down. You should be happy because all of these people came to see you and make you happy during your bereavement." It was later said that the speaker had hung diichaagh, or greatness, around the hostess's neck.

This speech fulfilled the speaker's reciprocal obligation to the hostess and her sib. It also reiterated an important feature of the potlatch exchange. With his words, he wrapped the hostess in love and respect, which, like the special potlatch blankets given to the close friends of the deceased, were supposed to warm her and lessen her grief. By telling her not to cheapen herself, he urged her to emulate her ancestors who, in effect, were represented by the power and prominence of Mount Sanford. By acknowledging the status of her ancestors, as well as her own, he sought to make her feel better and to emphasize the harmony and cooperation between moieties on this occasion.

On the day after the funeral, when everyone had again gathered in the hall, F.X., a Copper River man, dressed in a bright blue beaded chief's jacket, delivered a speech on etiquette. Speaking angrily in both the Ahtna language and English, he criticized as disrespectful the absence of the extended family members from the village after the body was brought back. They should have been in the village to greet the return of the body from Anchorage and to accept any condolences offered by attending members of the opposite moiety. Members of the opposite moiety from other Copper River villages should have been there as well. At this point, he pointedly excused several of the guests, including Jack, because they had to travel long distances. But he ignored others, specifically Elisha, who also had to travel a considerable distance. His rebuke caused no little tension and was immediately followed by a conciliatory speech in both Ahtna and English that was delivered by a tradition bearer from another Ahtna village. He said he was late because of family problems and transportation difficulties. Then R.M., a younger Ahtna man, made some further remarks in an effort to smooth over the increasing friction.

Elisha, speaking in both the Tanacross and the English language, responded to F.X.'s criticism. He prefaced his remarks by saying he was, at seventy-five, a little young to understand all this, a remark both self-effacing and designed to put the younger F.X. in his place. Elisha said he came to the potlatch to learn about the old time and about how people are related, and he thought everyone should forgive one another, not cause worry or bear hard feelings. All the same, he felt slighted that F.X. had not publicly excused him as he had others. No one had telephoned him, or the wrong person had been called. He had not known when the body came back to the village. The telephones were not working correctly so there was a mixup as to exactly when the body was to be returned to the village or when the funeral was to be held. In essence, Elisha said that if F.X. was going to be concerned with tradition, then he should follow traditional etiquette, which required that Elisha be contacted personally.[14] At the end of the speech, F.X. apologized to Elisha and tried to heal the breach by calling him brother.

Excusing Jack and ignoring Elisha had been a serious breach on F.X.'s part, insulting both Elisha and his wife, Lila. Their status entitled them to be contacted directly by the relatives of the deceased. By not doing so, the hosts had negated any obligation on the part of Lila or Elisha, who had fulfilled their respective obligations. As a member of the deceased's moiety, Lila had donated blankets and money to the potlatch and had come to share her relative's grief. Elisha, as a member of the moiety opposite that of the deceased, had been present when the grave was dug and had danced and sung and, as Lila's husband, had donated money to be used for food, which helped ensure the success of the potlatch. Since Elisha is a high-ranking member of the 'Al si' dEndi' sib, he should have been given recognition equal to Jack.

F.X.'s insult was not forgotten after the potlatch. The next week, Elisha discussed the insult with his first cousin, William, who had not attended the funeral, in terms of their family and sib. Although William, Elisha, and Jack belong to the same Naltsiin/'Al si' dEndi' sib, Jack's mother is from the Copper River while William's and Elisha's mothers are from Ketchumstuk. Consequently, their primary affiliations are with different maternal lineages of the same sib. By ignoring Elisha but recognizing Jack, F.X. had actually insulted Elisha's and William's maternal ancestors, a great insult indeed. Yet

Elisha had acted as a man of rank should. He had not given ground. He had a right to be angry, but he had put his anger aside in favor of maintaining the harmony of the potlatch.

Speeches such as those of F. X. and Elisha involve matters of etiquette and prestige. Others, delivered in English, are homilies aimed explicitly at the young and are filled with a sense of urgency and warning. At one potlatch in the summer of 1987, for example, William delivered such a speech. He said in English that he was forced to make a speech because the potlatch was important, that a speech had to be made for a potlatch. He said speeches were for teaching people about relationships, about who one is related to, about one's great ancestors. Speeches were also important for teaching the Indian way. He went on to criticize those who did not believe in the continuing importance of the potlatch.

Two inferences can be drawn from William's speech. Within the present context of relative abundance and the easy life afforded by the capitalist system, people should not mistake the meaning of the potlatch to be about things instead of people. This is why he stresses the importance of talking about relationships. Second, William's speech points directly to the ongoing internal dialogue about the importance of cultural tradition. He believes the potlatch retains its significance, a view derived, at least in part, from his very active involvement in land claims politics. To this end, William continually speaks, at potlatches and wherever he can, about the importance of the Indian way and the importance of the land.

Although William has been criticized for addressing political issues in the potlatch, there is no disagreement about the propriety of addressing homilies to the young about the Indian way. Older people feel that the young people are forgetting their culture. Echoing her brother William, Jean, during the same potlatch, expressed her concern over the young people forgetting their language and who they are. She said she was afraid that after the old people died, everyone would be "lost" and that Jack was the only one who could "hold" the people up. Jack, as the youngest of the elders, would be the only person left who knew how to lead the songs and dances and make speeches.

Similar sentiments were voiced by the former president of the Ahtna regional corporation who attended a potlatch at Tanacross in the fall of 1987. After thanking his hosts for inviting him and his people, he commented on how the Upper Tanana and Copper River people share each other's grief and are one family. He then said that losing the elders meant a loss of a "cultural resource." The people of the upper Tanana have to listen to William, he said, and be guided by him and his knowledge because sometime he will be gone.[15]

Gratitude speeches are often short, but they remove the potlatch from the mundane concerns of the changing social, political, and economic environment. In a speech of gratitude that Helen gave just before the distribution of gifts at her potlatch, she said, "It was for him," pointing to the picture of her son that was fastened to a Hudson's Bay-style blanket hung on the wall. "I have done all I can do. Now it is time to let him go. I cannot think about or worry about him anymore." She repeated this several times. She expressed her gratitude to both Natives and non-Natives who attended the potlatch and helped her. Eloquent and emotional, Helen shared her grief with her guests. And, by speaking English, she included non-Natives and younger people, thus breaking down, at least for the moment, some of the cultural and linguistic barriers separating the assembled guests.

DISTRIBUTION OF GIFTS

On the last night of a potlatch, the gifts, which had been stored in caches, are brought to the hall in pickup trucks and passed through a window, since the thresholds of the doors are considered to be polluted by young women passing through them. Although this precaution is redundant as young women are allowed into the hall, continuation of the tradition reemphasizes the spiritual nature of the gifts. Once in the hall, blanket after blanket, in every color imaginable, is removed from huge cloth storage bags and stacked in the center of the room.

Although symbolic of love and respect, the gifts, like food at the feasts, are amassed for calculated displays of abundance. At the potlatch for the old woman, whose funeral I discussed in chapter 6, there were between six hundred and seven hundred blankets stacked waist high in the center of the hall. Yet because most blankets are relatively inexpensive, their quantity is no indication of the size or expense of a potlatch. Rather, the social significance of a potlatch, as well as its size in economic terms, is measured by the number of guns, which are sometimes ostentatiously displayed.[16] At the funeral potlatch for the old woman there were forty rifles, which is considered a large potlatch.

After the gifts were stacked, Jack's daughter made a short speech to thank the guests. She said she hoped all the help (including the gifts) would be "blessed" and that she was happy people helped out because it really showed people cared for "grandma." She then read the names of people who made donations. The donations indicate people's affection for the deceased, and because of this the woman asked that they be blessed in the Christian sense. She also meant that the gifts be blessed to bring good luck to the hosts and attract other wealth so that those who made this potlatch eventually got back what they gave away.

At this potlatch a variety of individuals gave donations, including guns, blankets, cash, and food. Some of these donations are listed in table 3. The first collections of gifts were supplied by the deceased's closest maternal relative, her granddaughter, a member of the Dikagiyu sib. These included gifts accumulated by the granddaughter, donations made by members of her moiety, and donations from friends, like myself. As the basic payment to the opposite moiety for their participation in the funeral, the distribution of these gifts sustained reciprocity between moieties and by extension maintained traditional linkages between potential affines. This was also the focus of a second collection, consisting of five guns, contributed by the leading Dikagiyu woman in Tanacross. Her donations were meant to increase the size of the potlatch and thus enhance the prestige of her sib.

A third collection of gifts came from Jack's children, who are members of the deceased's Dikagiyu sib. The stated reason for distributing these gifts was not to honor the deceased but specifically to honor their father, who was saddened at the death of his aunt. In a general sense, these gifts served to maintain intermoiety reciprocity because they would be distributed to members of the opposite moiety. Their distribution was also meant to acknowledge specific matrilineal linkages between Jack's family and the guests. There were also two relatively large donations that were out of the ordinary because they were made by women in the moiety opposite to the deceased. The first was a collection of gifts supplied by a woman who had dressed the corpse. Her stated reason for providing these gifts was her distress at Jack's grief. A second

Table 3
Gifts Provided to a Potlatch in Tanacross
for a Dikagiyu Woman

Donor (Sib)	Items Donated	Relationship to Deceased
Female Dikagiyu	4 guns, 150 blankets, $300 cash	Granddaughter of the deceased. Gifts used as partial payment to opposite moiety.
Group of Siblings Dikagiyu	3 guns, $100 cash, 50 blankets	Gifts donated to honor their father who was the deceased's brother's son. Because these people were the same sib as the deceased, their donations could be used as payment to the opposite moiety.
Wife Dikagiyu Husband 'Al si' dEndi'	5 guns, $50 cash	Wife is a sibmate of the deceased. Guns used as payment to the opposite moiety. Cash from husband was used to purchase groceries.
Female 'Al si' dEndi'	4 guns, 50 blankets	Woman was a member of the moiety opposite to the deceased. This donation was made in honor of the deceased's brother's son who is a sibmate of the donor.

Table 3 continued

Donor (Sib)	Items Donated	Relationship to Deceased
Female 'Al si' dEndi'	2 guns, 20 blankets, $100 cash	Woman was a member of the moiety opposite the deceased. This donation was made in honor of the deceased who was the donor's paternal aunt.
Male Dikagiyu	$50 cash	Member of the same moiety as deceased. Gift was used as part of the payment to opposite moiety.
Male Dikagiyu	$100 cash	Member of the same sib as deceased.
Female Dikagiyu	5 blankets, 10 scarves	Member of the same sib as deceased.
Female Tc'a·z	10 blankets, 1 gun	Member of the same sib as deceased.
Female	5 blankets, $50 cash	Member of the same sib as deceased.
Female	21 blankets, $50 cash	Member of the same sib as deceased.

collection of gifts was made by Jack's daughter specifically for the deceased, who was her paternal aunt.

In effect, the distribution of gifts served to honor two people, the deceased, who was of the Dikagiyu sib, and Jack, her brother's son, a member of the opposite 'Al si' dEndi' sib. This was allowed because in Tanacross these two sibs are linked through exclusive marriages so that each reproduces and reinforces the other, creating two powerful localized lineages allied by many marriages. The deceased was the last surviving member of a group of siblings who, because they made these correct marriages, were the progenitors of almost every living Tanacross resident. Additionally, the deceased was Jack's last surviving relative on his father's side. Consequently, while the potlatch was technically hosted by the Dikagiyu, with the 'Al si' dEndi' as guests, members of the 'Al si' dEndi' sib took advantage of the situation to distribute gifts.

The distribution of gifts, listed in table 4, followed the general pattern that placed initial emphasis on moiety reciprocity and the age-structured hierarchy. The first people to receive gifts were the six ranking men and women of the opposite moiety. Acknowledgment of their rank and effort was apparent in the amount and kinds of gift they received. In this instance, they received a necklace, one gun, two blankets, and $20. Additionally, the deceased's son-in-law, a non-Native man who had taken care of her for many years, was given the same gifts. Many non-Native people closely attached to the village are thus publicly honored. When this was done, the crowd clapped to show their approval.

The second category of people to receive gifts were the young male members of the opposite moiety who dug the grave and acted as pallbearers. Their gifts differed from that of their elders in that instead of receiving a symbol of leadership or rank, such as a necklace, they were given a digging tool as a symbol of their labor. Again, to show their approval, both for the young men's participation and the gift,

Table 4
Major Gifts Distributed at a Potlatch in Tanacross
for a Dikagiyu Woman

Recipient	Role in Ceremony	Gifts Received	Relation to Host
Nesas	Sang, led pot-latch song	2 blankets, $20 cash	Elder in sib opposite from deceased
Male 'Al si' dEndi'	Danced and sang	Same as above	Elder in sib opposite from deceased
Male 'Al si' dEndi'	Made condolence speech, danced and sang	Same as above	Elder in sib opposite from deceased
Female 'Al si' dEndi'	Danced and sang	Same as above	Elder in sib opposite from deceased
Male 'Al si' dEndi'	Danced and sang	Same as above	Elder in sib opposite from deceased
Male 'Al si' dEndi'	Danced and sang	Same as above	Elder in sib opposite from deceased
Male	None	Same as above	White man, former grandson-in-law of the deceased
Male	Helped dig grave, danced and sang	Gun, 2 blankets, $20 cash, shovel	Young man in moiety opposite the deceased
Male	Helped dig grave	Gun, 2 blankets, $20 cash, rope used to lower coffin	Young man in moiety opposite the deceased
Male	Helped dig grave	Gun, 2 blankets, $20 cash, ax	Young man in moiety opposite the deceased

Table 4 continued

Recipient	Role in Ceremony	Gifts Received	Relation to Host
Male	Danced and sang	Gun, 2 blankets, $20 cash	Elder who traveled long distance
Male	Danced and sang	$20 cash, 4 blankets	Participant who traveled long distance
Female	Danced and sang	$20 cash, 4 blankets	Participant who traveled long distance

the audience clapped and cheered. Included in this round of distributions were two non-Native men who had helped during the funeral.

Once these distributions were finished, lower-ranking guests and visitors including the priest and missionary were given several blankets. Finally, once the bulk of the gifts had been distributed, the remainder were given out in a somewhat random fashion to anyone who had not yet received one. At this point, relatives of the deceased scanned the audience to make certain no one especially helpful was forgotten. However, to maintain moiety distinctions, none of the members of the deceased's sib received a gift, even if they participated in the funeral. Once the distribution ended, all those who received something danced with their gifts. Elated, the crowd danced one last dance, waving their gifts above their heads, demonstrating their appreciation for the gifts, and restating their solidarity. The potlatch was now officially over.

The ritual actions of the potlatch, structured by tradition, emphasize the values of love, respect, reciprocity, generosity, kinship, and competence. At the same time, these values and actions are used to mask statements of superiority in the distribution of food and gifts. Potlatch oratory, more than any other aspect of the ceremony, is a potent demonstration of the underlying tensions in the ceremony. Oratory can bring conflict into the open. Its tensions can be mediated by speeches in which the guests assuage the host's grief. With his words, the speaker wraps the host in love and respect and builds the host's confidence by talking about the strength and courage of the host's "great people," or relatives. In doing this, the speaker emphasizes the harmony and cooperation between the potlatch participants in the hope of cementing the unity of the group. Nevertheless, conflicts over prerogatives and prestige can erupt at any time. As we have seen, this can result in a verbal exchange as each speaker attempts to maintain his prestige or to soothe over bad feelings.

Feasting, dancing, singing, distributing gifts, all in large measure free of the hazards of speech, forcefully dramatize the most enduring Native values. In the feast, the host endeavors to create an image of abundance and demonstrate his competence as a provider. Sharing food with guests meets his reciprocal obligations. In keeping with tradition, the evening feast is served on the floor, in the old way, and is therefore a reminder of a period of history characterized by Native autonomy and competence.

Singing and dancing express grief, then joy. Sorry songs help to control and expel grief, while dance songs provide a release. Together they put in balance the forces that have been created at the death of a person. As part of the reciprocal obligations between host and guest, everyone is obliged to dance. With swelling emotion, everyone joins in a display of harmony that marks the potlatch. Singing and dancing lift the spirits, and they are instrumental in creating, if only for a few hours, a sense of communal solidarity.

The climax of every potlatch is the distribution of gifts. We have seen the lengths to which a host will go to accumulate resources for the ceremony. Through the distributions, the hosts seek to maintain reciprocal relations and to extend those relations by distributing gifts to as many people as possible. Such distributions speak to the importance of maintaining the fundamental relationships that are the basis for Tanacross society. At the same time, the distribution of gifts is an attempt to reformulate existing relations between Natives and non-Natives based on a model of equality and reciprocity. By accumulating and then distributing goods produced by the non-Natives, Tanacross people try to place non-Native economic success in a Native perspective. That is, by accumulating large numbers of objects, they believe they demonstrate their equality with non-Natives, which they then transform into a superiority by distributing them in a grand gesture of social solidarity. Within the present political and economic context, this gesture becomes an act of resistance against the assimilation and domination of Native society while at the same time asserting a commonality with non-Natives based on a perceived set of shared values: generosity and love. It is also a statement made by older Natives to younger Natives about what is correct and acceptable human behavior.

CHAPTER 8

Conclusion

The potlatch is the most significant cultural event in the life of the Tanacross people. Whereas the dead are buried with a Christian funeral service, people persist in expressing their grief through song and dance and the distribution of gifts. Likewise, they continue to gain prestige from putting on a potlatch, and those who lead as singers, drummers, orators, and organizers gain respect and prestige as tradition bearers. Through their ritual actions, Tanacross people also affirm continuity with their past and in so doing restate their identity as Native people.

I have broadly interpreted the meaning of the modern potlatch in terms of the dialectic between cooperation and competition and as a struggle to maintain and reproduce a cultural identity based on the collectivity of Native society as opposed to the individualization of Euro-American society. For some scholars, the dialectical relationship between cooperation and competition ended during the fur trade as local leaders began to individually compete for prestige by distributing trade goods in the potlatch. From this perspective, the social and spiritual underpinnings of the ceremony collapsed in a flood of material wealth symbolically unrelated to Athapaskan culture.

As we have seen, however, the meeting between the Tanacross people and the external world was mediated by a coherent symbolic system. The use of trade goods in the potlatch did not undermine the meaning of the ceremony. Rifles, blankets, and beads were each symbolically transformed into expressions of emotion and used to create and maintain vital social linkages. What is conveyed in modern potlatch gifts, then, is an affirmation of shared values based on reciprocal obligations that creates a web of fundamental social relationships. The host's prestige rests on his or her ability to sustain these relationships.

Similarly, although leadership changed as "old time" rich men lost their prominence in economic life, modern tradition bearers continue to be significant figures in village social and cultural life. They, like past leaders, compete individually for prestige through the display of traditional knowledge and the ability to mobilize and organize the people. At the same time, they, more than anyone else, are expected to reflect traditional values by placing the welfare of the community above self-interest and acting as cultural guides by urging adherence to the Indian way.

As a response to changes in their relationship with non-Natives, Tanacross people have constructed an identity based on an opposition in which competition symbolizes the white man's way and cooperation the Indian way. Native people see themselves as adhering to the traditional values of kinship, sharing, reciprocity, love and respect, and competence which are in opposition to the individualistic, self-centered values of non-Native society. As a model for action, however, the Indian way presents contradictory images. People see themselves as coming from a positive past but moving, almost inexorably, toward a negative future of alienation, economic competition, and materialism. The potlatch is a major anchor to that positive past.

As a mooring in a tide of change, the potlatch is considered immutable. In the funeral potlatch people act out reciprocal obligations that have structured traditional Athapaskan
life for generations. As they act out their responsibility in
caring for the corpse, building the coffin and grave fence, and
digging the grave, they demonstrate their competence as true
human beings as well. Through singing, dancing, oratory,
and the distribution of gifts and food, people also show their
love and respect for kin who form a web of relationships
extending far beyond the immediate family and village. In this
respect the central act of distribution is a key symbol of
resistance. By continuing to distribute accumulated goods,
Native people maintain a distinct image of themselves in
opposition to what they perceive as a self-centered and non-
reciprocating white society.

Viewed as a distinctly Athapaskan ritual, the potlatch
legitimates Tanacross culture through a display of tradition
that counteracts outward signs of change and general non-
Native racist stereotypes. Within the context of the potlatch,
Euro-American values lose ground to assertions and demonstrations of Athapaskan spirituality and community. Through
the ideal of cooperation, Native people attempt to create and
maintain a certain view of what is decent and acceptable
human behavior. And by encouraging and seeking the participation of non-Natives, Tanacross people look to re-create a
relationship with whites based on equality and reciprocity. In
this respect the potlatch does not simply mark or create ethnic
boundaries but attempts to subvert them.

The potlatch has survived a kaleidoscope of historical
change. Clearly, it serves a profound need in the human
endeavor to understand who one is. And in the context of
Tanacross culture, this is achieved within a framework of

ceremonial and social relations. As one man told me, "We have to stick together, otherwise who will bury us, who will make the [grave] fence? Someday, who knows, maybe I will make your fence."

Notes

INTRODUCTION

1. Part of this concept comes from Kan (1986). Guedon (1974: 129) writes that in the past there was a balance between a "strong individualism" and a "feeling of solidarity" which has been lost.

2. This concept is derived from Scott (1985: 23).

3. To what extent this occurred in Tanacross culture is unclear. For instance, McKennan (1959: 132), despite these developments, saw a weak leadership whose only claim lay in its continued ability to accumulate and distribute gifts. In fact, McKennan believed that as soon as a leader became unable to fulfill his duties, his position was immediately usurped. But this perception is unsupported by either historical evidence or ethnographic data (Allen 1887; Strong 1972; Kari 1986).

CHAPTER 1

1. For example, the Tc'I'tcElyu (or C'ecaely u in Ahtna and Tcitcelyu in Upper Tanana), the Naltsiin (Naltsiinn and Naltsina), the Dikagiyu (Dik'aagiyu and Dik'agiyu) and 'Al si' dEndi' (Alts'en'Tnaey and Altsetdendei) are all found among the Ahtna and Upper Tanana (Kari 1986; de Laguna 1975). Similarly, the Tc'I'tcElyu (Tcetcelyu), Nal tsin (NelchIn), and 'Al si' dEndi' (Atzitdinné) are found among the Middle Tanana and the Lower Tanana (de Laguna 1975).

CHAPTER 2

1. Russian and English attempts at redirecting the indigenous trade to their advantage were only partially successful. The Russians were most successful around Cook Inlet where they controlled the trade through superior force. Otherwise they were notably unsuccessful in western Alaska and along the Copper River (see Zagoskin 1967 and VanStone 1979 for a discussion on the trade in western Alaska). In the Yukon Territory, the Chilkat Tlingit destroyed the Hudson's Bay Company post at Fort Selkirk

and chased the trader, Robert Campbell, out of the country (see McClellan 1975 on the Yukon trade).

2. The isolation of the Upper Tanana Region is illustrated by the fact that the Tanacross and Upper Tanana languages have only 4 Russian loanwords in their vocabulary as compared to the Upper Ahtna dialect, which has 21, the Western Ahtna dialect, which has 62, and the Kenai dialect of Dena'ina which has about 350. The complexity and diversity of the trade is also suggested by the fact that the Upper Ahtna language has 3 French words derived from Slavey jargon and 3 Gwich'in words (Kari 1986).

3. As far as I know, there are no quantitative data on protocontact trade in this region of Alaska.

4. Although Dall (1870) indicates that Tanana River Natives visited Fort Yukon, there is no evidence that these were Tanacross or Upper Tanana people. McKennan (1959) believes that no people from the Upper Tanana River visited either Fort Selkirk or Fort Yukon.

5. McIntosh to Wood, March 5, 1917, Episcopal Church Archives, R.G. 62–42, folder 1.

6. McIntosh to Wood, March 5, 1917, Episcopal Church Archives, R.G. 62–42, folder 2.

7. Hajdukovich, Special Cases collection, 1932–33, National Archives, Bureau of Indian Affairs records, box 228.

8. Behind his humanitarian purpose, Hajdukovich's interest was in establishing a monopoly on the regional fur trade. He was successful in creating a reservation for the Tetlin people. After it was created the Natives established their own store and kept Hajdukovich out. Because of this, he abruptly dropped plans to establish a reservation at Tanacross. For a full account, see Brown (1984). Also see Halpin (1985: 11), who writes, "Although Hajdukovich's comments show concern for the people of Tetlin, it is unlikely that his intentions were purely altruistic. As the dominant trader in the area, it would certainly be in his best interest to 'safeguard' the region from potential competitors, and to sustain the trade by encouraging conservation of fur resources by his clientele."

9. These data come from a variety of sources, including Back 1930; Endicott 1928; Strong 1972; and the John Hajdukovich collection, University of Alaska at Fairbanks (UAF) Archives, box 3, and my field notes.

10. Hajdukovich collection, UAF Archives, box 3.

11. Snowshoe frames were made by men out of birch. Women customarily filled the frames in with babiche, a type of rawhide made out of untanned moose skin.

12. Hajdukovich collection, UAF Archives, box 3.

13. McIntosh to Wood, December 12, 1932, Episcopal Church Archives, R.G. 62–42, folder 2.

14. Interview conducted in Anchorage, November 1986.

15. Arthur Wright in Bishop Rowe's correspondence, 1927, Episcopal Church Archives, R.G. 62–61.

16. Veta McIntosh, R.G. 75, Dept. of Interior, Office of Indian Affairs, Annual School Reports of Alaska Schools, 1933–35. Annual School Report, July 20, 1933.

17. In 1946, construction began on the Taylor Highway, which winds its way through the hills of the Fortymile River country to Eagle and Dawson City. A number of people from Tanacross worked on the road, which was finished in 1954. This road had a particular effect on Tanacross subsistence activities because it bisected the migration route of the Forty-mile caribou herd, traditionally the main source of food for the Tanacross people, and made the herd accessible to "road hunters" from Fairbanks and Anchorage. It is believed that the Fortymile caribou herd began to decline after the construction of the Taylor Highway. There had been a significant decrease in the size of the herd since 1920, when the herd was estimated at 528,000 animals. By 1961, the herd had decreased to 60,000 animals; in the summer of 1975, to 8,610.

CHAPTER 3

1. In the late nineteenth and twentieth century, the Athapaskan economy in Alaska was both a consumer-based economy, in which hunters trapped for furs in order to purchase commodities, and a "gift economy," (Gregory 1982). In a gift economy, the idea of private property is limited and property is not alienated or considered separate from a person (Mauss 1967; Gregory 1982). Furthermore, consumption and exchange in a gift econo-my is "primarily concerned with the regulation of relations between people in the process of social and biological reproduction" (Gregory 1982: 79).

2. Nelson (1983) writes that the Koyukon Athapaskans believe all things possess a spirit. This spirit, I believe, can be compared to the Tlingit concept of yek, which is a constant personified spiritual power in an object or being (McClellan 1975: 68), or the Maori concept of hau, which is a "vital essence of life found in human beings, in land, and in things. Because the hau is connected through people to land and things, things take on the power of personification" (Weiner 1985: 212).

3. Apparently, this also means cars, television sets, videocassette players, coffee pots, and other consumer goods, although I never heard anyone say so. It certainly applies to commercially made clothes. It is considered bad luck, for example, for a wife to wear any of her husband's clothes (see Nelson 1983: 27 on Koyukon beliefs related to luck). McClellan (1975: 300) has also pointed out the intimate connection between individuals and their clothing. Nelson (1983: 27), writing about the Koyukon Athapaskan, says the Koyukon believe that possessions such as sleds, rifles, fishnets, and clothing possess luck that can either be taken away or given to someone else if they use your possessions.

4. The idea that the host gives something of value to sustain his guests is illustrated in a story about a potlatch held at Tetlin in the late nineteenth

or early twentieth century. The host invited people from Dawson City, in the Yukon Territory, and gave them several dozen marten skins as a potlatch gift because, according to my informant, the price of marten in the Dawson area was much higher than in Tetlin. The idea was that the Dawson people would benefit more from selling the skins than the host would.

5. The fact that the chief is called a "friend" to Tsiint-le' indicates he was not a relative but a partner and a member of the opposite moiety.

6. For two more versions of stories that relate how "dentalium necklaces came to the people," see Paul 1980. For another version of the bear story, see McKennan 1959.

7. Kan (1986) notes a similar significance for blankets in the Tlingit potlatch. The physical feeling of the soft, warm blanket conveyed warmth to the guests who thanked their hosts for "warming them."

8. At one potlatch I was given a piece of cloth as a joke. Now that I had a piece of cloth I was supposed to find a wife to give it to.

9. McKennan (1959) noted that immediately after a potlatch he attended in the Ahtna village of Batzulnetas in 1930, the guests began selling their gifts.

10. At one potlatch, commemorating the recovery of a young man from an accident, the man who stayed with him during the accident was given a beaded moose hide gun case and a rifle that he refused to sell.

11. Prices quoted are in 1987 U.S. dollars.

CHAPTER 4

1. McClellan (1975: 489) writes that the Tutchone also distinguish between elected chiefs and traditional chiefs.

2. James Fall (1987: 3) writes that an Upper Inlet Dena'ina leader can be best understood as a "rich man" who achieved status "through [his] skills in hunting, trapping, and trading and [his] use of material goods to create groups of economic and political supporters. Each man's position in the matrilineal kinship system, as well as reputed associations with manifestations of spiritual power, enhanced the likelihood that he could attain high rank. In sum, manipulation of material wealth, kinship ties and esoteric knowledge was the means by which individuals gained power." McClellan (1975) says that among the Tutchone the word "chief" translates to "man with lots of stuff" (489) and that chiefs were considered "high people" who could buy many things (490).

3. Whites are not allowed to run for the village council.

4. Chief Andrew Isaac died in March 1991. His successor to the position of traditional chief of the Doyon Region is Chief Peter John of Minto.

5. Some rich men had up to six wives and were considered "smart guys" who did not work but left that to their poorer relations and followers. The competition and jealousy between these men was said to have been considerable (McKennan collection, UAF Archives, box 6).

6. The importance of the chief and his place were reflected in the type of houses constructed. When an old man, that is, leader, decided to stay in a place for the winter, he directed his people to make a bark house. These large, semisubterranean structures could house a large family of several wives, children, and other relatives such as a chief would have. Bark houses were not only larger but more permanent than the more modest tepees built by lesser men.

7. Marianne Boelscher (pers. comm.), speaking of the Haida, says there are two aspects of rank. The first is a formal (or ascribed) aspect contingent on birth, one's ancestors, and how many potlatches one's ancestors have given. Another aspect, called by the Haida "fitness for respect," is based on a leader's social knowledge and ability to lead in rituals. This also includes knowledge of informal relationships.

8. The issue of whether sibs are ranked has been brought up by Heinrich (1957), who says they are. Certainly, in Tanacross, the Dikagiyu and Nal tsin/'Al si' dEndi' are considered the two highest-ranked sibs. Within the Upper Tanana Region, the Dikagiyu are considered the "millionaire tribe, high-priced people" as indicated previously (Guedon 1974: 69).

9. It must be remembered that we are talking about groups ranging from 10 to 50 people, if the earliest population figures have any validity.

10. Balikci's (1963: 62–63) description of Vunta Kutchin chiefs parallels that of the Upper Tanana leader. He writes that there is a "succession of polygynous tribal chiefs, economic leaders (owners of the caribou surrounds), moiety chiefs, war captains, religious leaders or shamans who acted on behalf of the whole community in crises periods."

11. At Ketchumstuk, there were several other clans including Tc'a·z, Naltsiin, or crow people (Guedon 1974); Al' si' dEndi', who were said to have come out of water weeds found around Midway Lake near Tetlin; the Dikagiyu; the Tcicyu; and the Tc'l'tcElyu. The Tc'l'tcElyu grandfather was from Flint Rock as well.

12. I believe the relationship between the Upper Ahtna and Mansfield people rested on creating marriage alliances for subsistence and trade reasons. The area just north of Mansfield is a major pathway for caribou migration and was utilized by the Upper Ahtna people at the invitation of their Mansfield partners. At the same time, the Copper River is home to major salmon runs, and it appears that Mansfield people may have gotten fish from the Upper Ahtna people. In the late eighteenth century and all through the nineteenth century, Copper River people had access to Russian and later American trade goods that came from Cook Inlet and Prince William Sound. These were traded north into Tanacross territory. In the 1880s, the trade was reversed when Americans built trading stations on the upper Yukon. One of the major trails linking the Copper, Tanana, and Yukon rivers went by the village of Mansfield.

13. One fence was near the Little Dennison River, one at a place called Wolf Creek, another located in the vicinity of present Tok Junction, and a

fourth at a place called Soldagarten (Soldier's Garden) near Tanacross. This last fence Sam Thomas built near the end of his life when he was blind and lived in the mission village of Tanacross. Apparently, this fence was rather short and used to snare both moose and caribou. The snares were said to be made from old telegraph wire.

14. The Reverend F. B. Drane wrote in 1918 that "it is a day when the people are looking for a new leader." He went on to say that "here at Saint Timothy's they see that the cause of right is upheld and that even the most powerful man of the old caste is rebuked when he advocates some unjust measure. They [Native people] see that each man is given a fair consideration and that prominence does not make him more favored." Furthermore, the "child-like nature of our Indians makes them naturally look up for leadership. Many of their former chiefs were strong men, but in most cases they held their power as medicine men. Now when the young people see how kind and impartial are the mission ways of doing things they take eagerly to our counsels." (Drane, *Spirit of Missions* 83, no. 3 (March 1918): 190).

15. Guedon (1974: 230) recorded a potlatch speech in which the speaker said there were four ways to go: hell, heaven, Indian, and white.

CHAPTER 5

1. Savishinsky (1970) has isolated similar values for the Hare. He writes that they place strong emphasis on kinship ties, generosity, and emotional restraint. Similar conceptions of "Indianness" have been reported by Lithman (1984: 167), who has formalized them into an "opposition ideology."

2. Finally, when the interview was over and I began to write a few notes, he exclaimed, "Now I was going to make some money off of him!" (Interview at Tanacross, Dec. 1986).

3. These broader changes include such diverse elements as the feminist movement, drugs, the American Indian Movement (AIM), political conservatism, and Christian fundamentalism.

4. It is difficult to generalize about these divisions in terms of the age of any one individual. The man who felt Native culture was only concerned about the past and compared the village to a corral is in his mid-fifties. Although he has lived in Fairbanks for over twenty years, he frequently returns to the village and is considered to be extremely competent in the woods. In contrast, one of my most knowledgeable associates, who taught me much about the potlatch, is a man in his thirties who never hunts or traps. There are also a number of old people who do not participate in anything "traditional." Likewise, most teenage boys do not participate in traditional activities such as the potlatch, but several do hunt and trap and have varying degrees of bush knowledge.

5. People leave the village for various reasons: military service, high school at the BIA school in Chemawa, Oregon, vocational training, or

university. Three young people, who are now in school, said they will join the military when they have completed their studies so they can get out of the village. The young lady said she wanted to join the air force to get away from the village. She would like to come home on the weekends but not live there.

6. Paraphrased from field notes.

7. This contemporary Native image of equality is in stark contrast to the image missionaries presented at the time. In November 1931, the missionary E. A. McIntosh wrote that the traders combined "and are going to squeeze the people proper this winter. One of them is U.S. Commissioner [Hajdukovich] and he says he is going to levy on everything they have for their debts. He says some of them owe as much as $800.00 and he is going to collect" (McIntosh correspondence, Episcopal Church Archives, R.G. 62–42, folder 7, 1930–39). Here the Indians are portrayed not as equals but as debtors or victims, about to be squeezed by the evil trader.

8. Miners used to hang their meat, and it sometimes dried out and acquired a particular taste that the miners did not like but the Native people did.

9. From tape-recorded interview at Tanacross, Oct. 1988.

10. The Episcopal Church continued to provide a priest at Tanacross until the 1960s. During the 1950s, the Reverend Bob Green served at Tanacross. Because Green was able to help the village through the postwar transition, he had a profound impact, and today he is remembered in almost mythical terms. His most important contribution, I think, was his attempt to bridge the widening gap between the Native and white communities. But he also fostered, either consciously or unconsciously, the traditional paternalistic attitudes of the Church.

11. From a tape-recorded interview at Tanacross, Oct. 1988.

12. Braroe (1975: 151) writes that Plains Cree criticize all whites for being miserly and unwilling to extend help. Whites "don't take care of anybody, just take care of themselves. Indians different. We care for each other, share what we got."

13. The literature on the kinship of Athapaskan people living on the upper Tanana River consists of McKennan's discussion (1959, 1969), an article by Heinrich (1957), and Guedon's published dissertation (1974).

14. Guedon (1974: 87) reports a similar situation in Tetlin where the Dikagiyu and Nal tsin have intermarried for several generations.

15. Historically, a number of ceremonies were held which involved the reciprocal exchange of gifts, like the winter ceremony (McKennan 1959; Guedon 1974), which has been replaced by a Christmas festival that includes an exchange of gifts. Like the winter ceremony, this exchange is not based on moiety or sib affiliation but on village membership, and the names of gift recipients are pulled out of a hat.

16. Native people's patriotism is reflected in their veneration for the American flag and the colors red, white, and blue. The flag, for example,

was used as a sign of leadership and strength by the Mansfield people. Today a man who makes dance sticks often uses red, white, and blue because he wants to identify with something strong, that is, America.

17. I am aware of several instances when young white hitchhikers were brought into the village and given a meal, clothes, and some money.

18. Paraphrased from field notes recorded in Tanacross, 1987.

19. Paraphrased from field notes recorded in Tanacross, 1987.

20. Competition is now really between Natives and whites. Although competition continues to be an aspect of the potlatch, as we shall see later, the major competition is now over land and resources and pits Native against non-Native. The Indian way becomes one weapon in this competition and is thus a particular type of "Native" tool. Ridington (1987) states that the Prophet Dance of the Beaver is a particular Indian way of dealing with adaptive change brought about by contact.

21. "Overflow glaciers" occur when the stream freezes and water flows over the top of the ice and over the banks of the stream. Apparently, the hunters sank into the deep snow, even with their snowshoes on, and they could move faster on the ice. They could not use snowshoes on overflow ice; the ice would break the snowshoe frames.

CHAPTER 6

1. The term "grandma" is classificatory and refers to all old people above the paternal generation regardless of sib affiliation.

2. This celebration was reported, accompanied by photographs, in an Anchorage newspaper. Celebrations are frequently held to honor significant elders in the community. The village of Northway has a birthday party every year for its chief, Walter Northway, which is attended not only by local people but by Natives and non-Natives from Anchorage and Fairbanks. The party has been reported in the Anchorage and Fairbanks newspapers as well as the Doyon region newsletter. In 1981, there was a potlatch in Tanacross for Andrew Isaac, the "traditional chief" of the Doyon Region, which was attended by a number of local and regional politicians.

3. In 1975, the village of Minto put on a potlatch and killed a cow moose to feed the guests. Carlos Frank, one of the young men involved in the hunt, was arrested and convicted in district court for the unlawful transportation of a moose illegally taken. Frank appealed his conviction to the Alaska Supreme Court, which overturned the lower court's ruling, in 1979. The Supreme Court ruled that "the use of moose meat at religious funeral ceremony was a practice deeply rooted in defendant's religion and that the defendant was sincere in his religious beliefs." Further, the "state did not meet its burden of proving compelling state interest which would justify curtailing the religiously based practice" (Alaska, 604 P2d 1068).

4. Transfer payments received by people in the village include Aid to Families with Dependent Children (AFDC) given to single parents and

grandparents responsible for their grandchildren; social security payments; Supplemental Security Income (SSI), which supplements social security; an Alaska longevity bonus given to people over age 65 who have lived in Alaska for 25 consecutive years, which was $200 a month in 1980; food stamps, available to those below a certain income average; energy assistance, which was a single payment in 1980 varying between $250 and $400 (Haynes 1980: 34); unemployment insurance; an Alaska Permanent Fund Dividend, which is a single payment varying from year to year (in 1982, the payment was $1,000 for each man, woman and child; in 1988 the dividend was over $800); a village corporation annual dividend and an annual dividend from Doyon Ltd., the regional Native corporation organized under the Alaska Native Land Claims Settlement Act.

5. In some circumstances such as an unexpected death, transfer payments are used to cover immediate expenditures. In the case of funeral potlatches, they can also be used for donations, some people's donations being contingent on whether they get their "check" on time.

6. Paraphrased from field notes recorded in Tanacross, 1987.

7. I did not count the number of HBC blankets given away.

8. Guns in the Copper River region cost more. People from the Copper River charge $200 for a gun bought at a potlatch, rather than $175.

CHAPTER 7

1. Tanner (1974) describes a parallel relationship among an Algonkian group.

2. This food was introduced by and shared with "old whites." It is a historical link between Natives and whites and indicative of their once close relationship.

3. Both McKennan (1959) and Guedon (1974) record that a guest's participation in the potlatch is done as a favor to the host because he cares.

4. A story illustrates this point. Several years ago, there was a funeral potlatch held at Northway and the people danced, but they "couldn't break out the good time." Suddenly someone rushed into the hall and said there was some trouble outside. Everyone went out to find one whole family asphyxiated in their car right in front of the hall. After the dead were taken care of, all the people went back into the hall and danced really hard and were finally able to break the spell of bad luck. After this, everything was all right. (Story recorded at Northway, July 1987.)

5. Grief seems to have been less constrained in the past. When a person was told of the death of one of his relatives, he was watched carefully. Sometimes the messenger threw his arms around the person, pinioning his arms so that if his grief overcame him, he would not hurt himself. In grief, a mourner might cut himself or herself with knives and singe his or her hair in open fires.

6. Kan (1986: 200), noting similar expressions of grief among the Tlingit, writes that four special "crying songs" were sung, followed by four prolonged OO sounds, which are said "to expel sadness."

7. Guedon (1974) records that these same songs were sung at a potlatch she attended in Tetlin in 1969.

8. According to oral history, the Han, who live on the Yukon River to the north of Tanacross, introduced new dances to the Tanacross people in the form of "war" dances. Moosehide, the Han village near present-day Dawson City (Yukon Territory), was called the "headquarters" for dance, and the chief of Moosehide and his younger brother, whose name was Esau, were said to have practiced their dancing in front of a big mirror and "danced like spruce hen on the hillside, no different." This infusion shaped the Tanacross potlatch into the ceremony it is today and developed a whole new aspect characterized by active and vibrant dancing, indicating a celebration of life juxtaposed to the stately grieving of the mourning laments. (From an interview taped at Dot Lake, Alaska, Feb. 1987).

9. The production of these costumes was part of the Indian Education program funded by the U.S. government, which also allocated money for local people to teach Native culture in the school. While classes in the Tanacross language languished, it was the dancing and singing that, as a much more conspicuous activity that can be performed for non-Natives, has survived. During the 1970s, Tanacross dancers traveled to various southern cities to dance, and in 1987, they were recruited by the Tanana Chiefs Conference to dance in Washington, D.C., in support of amendments to ANCSA.

10. Emphasis on village affiliation is also a result of external pressures, particularly ANCSA, which created the village corporations.

11. Guedon (1974: 219) calls it the "lucky song."

12. In fact, it appears that a village is not really considered a village, or place of importance, if it does not have a sacred hill or mountain attached to it. Kari (1986: 13) writes that "each major village has (or had) a hill or mountain that is regarded as sacred. These sacred places serve as ever-present symbols of the people's ties to their land and their ancestors." According to de Laguna (1975: 91), these "landmarks" are "honored in potlatch songs and oratory as the 'grandfather's face' of the village people." She goes on to say that these "remind us of the Tlingit landmark crests, though Athna hills belong to the whole community, not to a sib. Individuals also have a sense of attachment to the places which have been the homes of their maternal 'grandmothers.'"

13. These lines were translated from the Tanacross language by Alice Brean. The breaks indicate normal patterns of Athapaskan speech. (Recorded at Dot Lake in February 1987.)

14. Guedon (1974: 211) writes that the ideal way in which to invite important people to a potlatch is to send one or two messengers to the "chiefs" and older people.

15. During a Tetlin potlatch held in 1969, Guedon (1974: 230) recorded this speech:

> When I'll die, you will put that one, drum stick, in my grave. Don't forget.
> You have to learn Indian ways. You speak English; have to speak Indian too. Me, I don't go to school too much, but I know Indian language. Know your ways. White man got his way. But you got to learn Indian ways. Don't forget.
> They are two ways. Indian way. White ways. Four ways altogether: Hell, heaven, white and Indian. We don't want to be stuck in the middle.
> Nobody wants to go to hell! [everybody laughs] All you remember the Bible, what Bible says. Some houses I feel sorry for them. People drink too much. Don't do it. No good that way. Don't forget your own ways. Have a good time, dance, dance. That's why you are here. Make happy.

16. In the 1920s and 1930s, both blankets and guns were hung outside on specially made fences. During the early 1970s, all the guns to be distributed at a potlatch were hung on the wall of the community hall throughout the entire three-day period of the potlatch. This practice has been discontinued because, as one woman said, someone might steal them. At a potlatch held in the fall of 1987, the children and grandchildren of the deceased paraded single file into the hall holding two rifles, each one wrapped with a dentalium shell necklace.

Bibliography

Alaska Department of Labor. 1991. *Alaska Population Overview—1990 Census and Estimates*. Juneau, Alaska.

Allen, H. T. 1887. *Report on an Expedition to the Copper, Tanana and Koyukuk Rivers in the Territory of Alaska, in the year 1885*. Washington, D.C.

Anderson, L. D. 1956. *According to Mama*. Edited by Audrey Loftus. Fairbanks: St. Matthew's Episcopal Guild.

Arnold, R. 1976. *Alaska Native Land Claims*. Anchorage: Alaska Native Foundation.

Back, E. J. 1930. *Report of Official Visit to Upper Tanana and Copper River Valleys Dec. 28, 1929 to Feb. 14, 1930*. Washington, D.C.: U.S. Department of Interior, Office of Education, National Archives.

Balikci, A. 1963. "Family Organization of the Vunta Kutchin." *Arctic Anthropology* 1(2): 62–69.

Bentley, J. B. 1943. "The Annual Report of the Rt. Rev. Jno. B. Bentley." *Alaskan Churchman*, February 1943.

Bently, G. C. 1987. "Ethnicity and Practice." *Comparative Studies in Society and History* 29(1): 24–55.

Bishop, C. 1983. "Limiting Access to Limited Goods: The Origins of Stratification in Interior British Columbia." In *The Development of Political Organization in Native North America, 1979 Proceedings of the American Ethnological Society*, ed. E. Tooker, 148–61. Washington, D.C.: American Ethnological Society.

———. 1987. "Coast-Interior Exchange: The Origins of Stratification in Northwestern North America." *Arctic Anthropology* 24(1): 72–83.

Braroe, N. W. 1975. *Indian and White: Self-Image and Interaction in a Canadian Plains Community*. Stanford: Stanford University Press.

Brown, M. C. 1984. *Indians, Traders and Bureaucrats in the Upper Tanana District: A History of the Tetlin Reserve.* Anchorage: Bureau of Land Management.

Capps, S. R. 1916. *The Chisana–White River District, Alaska.* U.S. Geological Survey, Bulletin no. 630. Washington, D.C.

Case, D. 1984. *Alaska Natives and American Laws.* University of Alaska Press. Fairbanks, Alaska.

Caulfield, R. A. 1992. "Alaska's Subsistence Management Regimes." *Polar Record* 28(164): 23–32.

Cole, T. M. 1979. *Historic Use of the Chisana and Nabesna Rivers, Alaska.* Unpublished report. State Department of Natural Resources, Juneau, Alaska.

Cook, J. 1989. "Historic Archaeology and Ethnohistory at Healy Lake, Alaska." *Arctic* 42(2): 109–18.

Cruikshank, J. 1985. "The Gravel Magnet: Some Social Impacts of the Alaska Highway on Yukon Indians." In *The Alaska Highway: Papers of the Fortieth Anniversary Symposium,* ed. Kenneth Coats, 172–87. Vancouver: University of British Columbia Press.

———. 1990. *Life Lived Like a Story: Life Stories of Three Yukon Native Elders.* Lincoln: University of Nebraska Press.

Dall, W. H. 1870. *Alaska and Its Resources.* Boston: Lee and Shepard.

Debo, A. 1970. *A History of the Indians of the United States.* Norman: University of Oklahoma Press.

de Laguna, F. 1975. "Matrilineal Kin Groups in Northwestern North America." In *Proceedings: Northern Athapaskan Conference, 1971,* ed. A. McFadyen Clark, I: 17–145. Ottawa: National Museums of Canada.

de Laguna, F., and McClellan, C. 1981. "Ahtna." In *Handbook of North American Indians.* Vol. 6, *Subarctic,* ed. J. Helm, 641–63. Washington, D.C.: Smithsonian Institution.

Drane, F. B. 1918. "A Cry in the Wilderness." *Spirit of Missions* 83(3): 189–91 (March).

Ellanna, L. J., and A. Balluta. 1992. *Nuvendaltin Quht'ana: The People of Nondalton.* Washington, D.C.: Smithsonian Institution Press.

Endicott, H. W. 1928. *Adventures in Alaska and Along the Trail.* New York: F. A. Stokes.

Fall, J. 1987. "The Upper Inlet Tanaina. *Anthropological Papers of the University of Alaska* 12(1–2): 1–80.

Fienup-Riordan, A. 1986. "The Real People: The Concept of Personhood Among the Yup'ik Eskimos of Western Alaska." *Etudes/Inuit/Studies* 10(1–2): 261–70.

——. 1992. *Culture Change and Identity Among Alaska Natives: Regaining Control*. Anchorage: Institute of Social and Economic Research, University of Alaska.

Goldman, I. 1975. *The Mouth of Heaven: An Introduction to Kwakiutl Religious Thought*. New York: Wiley.

Goldschmidt, W. 1946. *Delimitation of Possessory Rights of the Villages of Tetlin, Tanacross and Northway Interior Alaska*. Unpublished report for the Bureau of Indian Affairs.

Graves, M. 1913. "Saint Timothy's." *Alaska Churchman*, May 1913. 72–74.

Gregory, C. M. 1982. *Gifts and Commodities*. London: Academic Press.

Griffith, C. E. 1900. "From Knik Station to Eagle City." In *Compilation of Narratives of Explorations in Alaska*, 724–33. Washington, D.C.: U.S. Government Printing Office.

Gualtieri A. R. 1980. "Indigenization of Christianity and Syncretism among the Indians and Inuit of the Western Arctic." *Canadian Ethnic Studies* 12: 47–57.

Guedon, M-F. 1974. *People of Tetlin Why Are You Singing?* National Museum of Man, Mercury Series, Ethnology Division, Paper no. 9. Ottawa, Canada.

——. 1981. "Upper Tanana River Potlatch." In *Handbook of North American Indians*. Vol. 6, *Subarctic*, ed. J. Helm, 557–81. Washington, D.C.: Smithsonian Institution.

Hajdukovich, J. 1931–32. Hajdukovich Collection, box 3. University of Alaska Archives, Fairbanks, Alaska.

——. 1931–32. General Correspondence, R.G. 75, box 228, Special Cases. National Archives, Washington, D.C.

Halpin, L. 1985. *Living off the Land: A Study of Contemporary Patterns of Subsistence in Tetlin Alaska*. M.A. thesis, Department of Anthropology, University of Washington, Seattle.

Hardisty, W. 1872. "The Loucheaux Indians. In *Smithsonian Institution Annual Report for the Year 1866*, 311–20. Washington, D.C.: Smithsonian Institution.

Haycox, S. n.d. *Circumstances and Conditions of Military Airfield and Highway Construction at Tanacross Village, Alaska, 1942*. Unpublished paper, University of Alaska, Anchorage.

Haynes, T. 1980. *Aging in the Upper Tanana Region: An Assessment of Current Programs and the Needs of Older Alaskans*. Tok, Alaska:

Upper Tanana Development Corporation and Upper Tanana Aging Program.

Heinrich, A. 1957. "Sib and Social Structure on the Upper Tanana." In *Science in Alaska. Proceedings of the 8th Alaska Science Conference, Alaska Division,* 10–22. American Association for the Advancement of Science, Anchorage, Alaska.

Kan, S. 1983. "Words that Heal the Soul: Analysis of the Tlingit Potlatch Oratory." *Arctic Anthropology* 20(2): 47–59.

———. 1986. "The 19th-Century Tlingit Potlatch: A New Perspective." *American Ethnologist* 13(2): 191–212.

———. 1987a. "Memory Eternal: Orthodox Christianity and the Tlingit Mortuary Complex." *Arctic Anthropology* 24(1): 32–55.

———. 1987b. "Introduction. Native Cultures and Christianity in Northern North America: Selected Papers from a Symposium." *Arctic Anthropology* 24(1): 1–7.

———. 1989. *Symbolic Immortality: The Tlingit Potlatch of the Nineteenth Century.* Washington, D.C.: Smithsonian Institution Press.

Kari, J. 1986. *The Headwaters People's Country: Narratives of the Upper Ahtna Athabaskans.* Alaska Native Language Center, University of Alaska, Fairbanks.

Ketz, J. A. 1983. *Paxson Lake: Two Nineteenth-Century Ahtna Sites in the Copper River Basin, Alaska.* Anthropology and Historic Preservation Cooperative Studies Unit,. University of Alaska, Fairbanks.

Krauss, M., and V. Golla. 1981. "Northern Athapaskan Languages." In *Handbook of North American Indians.* Vol. 6, *Subarctic,* ed. J. Helm, 67–85. Washington, D.C.: Smithsonian Institution.

Lithman, Y. G. 1984. *The Community Apart: A Case Study of a Canadian Indian Reserve Community.* Winnipeg: University of Manitoba Press.

Loyens, W. J. 1964. "The Koyukon Feast for the Dead." *Arctic Anthropology* 2(2): 133–48.

McClellan, C. 1964. "Culture Contacts in the Early Historic Period in Northwestern North America." *Arctic Anthropology* (2)2: 3–14.

———. 1975. *My Old People Say: An Ethnographic Survey of the Southern Yukon Territory.* 2 vols. National Museum of Man, Publication in Ethnology, no. 6. Ottawa, Canada.

McIntosh, E. A. 1918. "A Big Feast at Tanana Crossing." *Alaska Churchman,* February, 1918, 47–49.

————. 1932. Letter written to Guy Madara, July 5, 1932. Episcopal Church Archives, R.G. 62–42, folder 7, 1930–39. Austin, Texas.

————. 1941. "St. Timothy's Mission, Tanacross." *Alaska Churchman,* August 1941, 3–12.

————. n.d. "St. Timothy's Mission, Tanacross, Alaska." Unpublished manuscript, University of Alaska Archives, Fairbanks.

McKennan, R. A. 1959. *The Upper Tanana Indians,* Yale University Publications in Anthropology, no. 59. New Haven, Connecticut.

————. 1962. Field Notes, box 6. acc. 85–098. University of Alaska Archives, Fairbanks.

————. 1962. "Tanana 1962 Duplicate Field Notes," box 15. acc. 85–098. University of Alaska Archives, Fairbanks.

————. 1969. "Athapaskan Groupings and Social Organization in Central Alaska." In *Band Societies,* ed. D. Damas. National Museums of Canada, Bulletin 228, Paper no. 4. Ottawa, Canada.

————. 1981. "Tanana," In *Handbook of North American Indians.* Vol. 6, *Subarctic,* ed. J. Helm, 562–76. Washington, D.C.: Smithsonian Institution.

McNabb, S. 1991. "Elders, Inupiat Ilitqusiat, and Cultural Goals in Northwest Alaska." *Arctic Anthropology* 28(2): 63–76.

Marcotte, J.R. 1991. Wildfish and Game Harvest and Use by Residents of Five Upper Tanana Communities, Alaska, 1987–88. Alaska Department of Fish & Game, Division of Subsistence, Technical paper 168. Juneau, Alaska.

Mauss, M. 1967. *The Gift.* New York: W. W. Norton.

Melchoir, H. R. 1987. "Alaska." In *Wild Furbearer Management and Conservation in North America,* ed. Milan Novak, James A. Baker, Martyn E. Obbard and Bruce Malloch, 1121–1127. Toronto: Ontario Ministry of Natural Resources.

Mercier, F. X. 1986. *Recollections of the Yukon: Memoirs from the Years 1868–1885.* Translated and edited by Linda F. Yarborough. Alaska Historical Commission Studies in History, no. 188. Alaska Historical Commission, Anchorage.

Michler, C. 1986. *Born with the River: An Ethnography and Ethnohistory of Alaska's Big Delta–Goodpaster Indians.* Alaska Department of Natural Resources, Division of Geological and Geophysical Surveys, Anchorage.

Moorehouse, T. 1989. *Rebuilding the Political Economies of Alaska Native Villages.* Institute of Social and Economic Research, University of Alaska, Anchorage.

Murdock, G P. 1960. *Social Structure*. New York: Macmillan.

Murie, O. J. 1921. Fish and Wildlife Service Field Reports (1887–1961), series 1, box 10, folder 13. Smithsonian Archives, Washington, D.C.

Murray, A. H. 1910. *Journal of the Yukon, 1847–1848*. Edited by L. J. Burpee. Publications of the Canadian Archives, no. 4. Ottawa, Canada.

Myers, F. 1986. *Pintupi Country, Pintupi Self: Sentiment, Place, and Politics among the Western Desert Aborigines*. Washington, D.C.: Smithsonian Institution Press.

Nelson, R. 1969. *Hunters of the Northern Ice*. Chicago: University of Chicago Press.

———. 1983. *Make Prayers to the Raven*. Chicago: University of Chicago Press.

Osgood, C. 1971. *The Han Indians*. Yale University Publications in Anthropology, no. 16. New Haven, Conn.

Paul, D. 1974. *According to Papa*. Fairbanks: St. Matthew's Episcopal Guild.

Paul, G. 1980. *Stories for My Grandchildren*. Transcribed and edited by Ron Scollon. Alaska Native Language Center, University of Alaska, Fairbanks.

Preston, R. 1975. *Cree Narrative: Expressing the Personal Meaning of Events*. National Museum of Man, Mercury Series, Ethnology Division, Paper no. 30. Ottawa, Canada.

Preston, S. 1986. *Let the Past Go: A Life History Narrated by Alice Jacob*. National Museum of Man, Mercury Series, Ethnology Division, Paper no. 104. Ottawa, Canada.

Ridington, R. N. 1988. *Domination and Cultural Resistance: Authority and Power among an Andean People*. Durham: Duke University Press.

———. 1987. "From Hunt Chief to Prophet: Beaver Indian Dreams and Christianity." *Arctic Anthropology* 24(1): 8–18.

Ridington, R. 1988. "Knowledge, Power, and the Individual in Subarctic Hunting Society." *American Anthropologist* 90: 98–110.

Ringel, G. 1979. "The Kwakiutl Potlatch: History, Economics and Symbols." *Ethnohistory* 26: 347–62.

Rowe, P. T. 1910–11. "Report of the Bishop of Alaska." In *The Annual Report of the Board of Missions of the Protestant Episcopal Church in the United States of America*, 67–68.

Sahlins, M. 1972. *Stone Age Economics*. London: Tavistock.

Savishinsky, J. S. 1970. "Kinship and the Expression of Values in an Athapaskan Bush Community." *Western Canadian Journal of Anthropology* 2(1): 31–59.

Schwimmer, E. 1972. "Symbolic Competition." *Anthropologica* 14: 117–55.

Scott, J. 1985. *Weapons of the Weak: Everyday Forms of Peasant Resistance.* New Haven: Yale University Press.

Sherwood, M. 1981. *Big Game in Alaska: A History of Wildlife and People.* New Haven: Yale University Press.

Simeone, W. E., and James VanStone. 1986. "'And He Was Beautiful': Contemporary Athapaskan Material Culture in the Collections of Field Museum of Natural History." *Fieldiana: Anthropology*, n.s. 10: 1–108. Chicago, Illinois.

Stearns, M. L. 1975. "Life Cycle Rituals of the Modern Haida." In *Contributions to Canadian Ethnology*, ed. David B. Carlisle, 129–69. National Museum of Man, Mercury Series, Ethnology Division. Ottawa, Canada.

Strong, B. S. 1972. *A History of Mentasta.* M.A. thesis, McGill University, Montreal, Quebec.

Stuck, H. 1913. "A Flying Visit to the Tanana Crossing." *Alaska Churchman*, May 1913, 83–86.

————. 1917. *Voyages on the Yukon and Its Tributaries: A Narrative of Summer Travel in Interior Alaska.* New York: Charles Scribner's Sons.

Tanner, A. 1974. "The Hidden Feast: Eating and Ideology among the Mistassini Cree." In *Papers of the Sixth Algonquian Conference*, ed. W. Cowan. National Museum of Man, Mercury Paper, Ethnology no. 23. Ottawa, Canada.

Townsend, J. 1965. *Ethnohistory and Culture Change of the Iliamna Tanaina.* Ph.D. dissertation, Department of Anthropology, University of California, Los Angeles.

————. 1975. "Mercantilism and Societal Change: An Ethnohistoric Examination of Some Essential Variables." *Ethnohistory* 22(1): 21–32.

Turner, V. 1974. *Dramas, Fields and Metaphor: Symbolic Action in Human Society.* Ithaca: Cornell University Press.

VanStone, J. W. 1979. "Ingalik Contact Ecology: An Ethnohistory of the Lower-Middle Yukon 1790–1935." *Fieldiana: Anthropology* 71: 1–273. Chicago, Illinois.

Weiner, B. A. 1985. "Inalienable Wealth." *American Ethnologist* 12: 210–27.

Wrangell, F. P. [1839] 1970. *Russian America: Statistical and Ethnographic Information.* Translated by Mary Sadouski. Materials for the Study of Alaska History, no. 15. Kingston, Ont.: Limestone Press.

Wright, A. 1925. "St. Timothy's Mission at Tanana Crossing, Alaska." *Spirit of Missions* 90(3): 172–73.

———. 1927. Typescript of article entitled "St. Timothy's Mission." R.G. 62–61, Bishop Rowe's Correspondence, 1927. Episcopal Church Archives, Austin, Texas.

Yarber, Y., and C. Madison, ed. and comps. 1988. *Andrew Isaac.* Central Alaska Curriculum Consortium. Fairbanks.

Zagoskin, L. A. 1967. *Lieutenant Zagoskin's Travels in Russian America, 1842–1844.* Edited by H. N. Michael. Arctic Institute of North America, Anthropology of the North, Translations from Russian Sources, no. 7. University of Toronto Press, Toronto.

Index